Learning with 'e's

Educational theory and practice in the digital age

Generated by Steve Wheeler

Foreword by Richard Gerver

Crown House Publishing Limited

First published by
Crown House Publishing
Crown Buildings, Bancyfelin, Carmarthen, Wales, SA33 5ND, UK
www.crownhouse.co.uk
and
Crown House Publishing Company LLC
6 Trowbridge Drive, Suite 5, Bethel, CT 06801-2858, USA
www.crownhousepublishing.com

© Steve Wheeler, 2015

First published 2015.

British Library of Cataloguing-in-Publication Data
A catalogue entry for this book is available from the British Library.

Print ISBN 978-1-84590-939-0
Mobi ISBN 978-1-84590-960-4
ePub ISBN 978-1-84590-961-1
ePDF ISBN 978-1-84590-962-8

LCCN 2014958781

Printed and bound in the UK by
Gomer Press, Llandysul, Ceredigion

Contents

Acknowledgements

I would like to thank the many members of my personal learning network for the inspiration to write this book. I would also like to thank my colleagues at Plymouth University and elsewhere for their support, for reading my blog and commenting, and for generally being there as a sounding board for my ideas. Lastly, I wish to thank my wife Dawn, and my family for their constant support and encouragement.

Foreword by Richard Gerver

We Woz There ...

I first met Steve Wheeler on a camel, by a Bedouin encampment, in the desert on the outskirts of Riyadh, Saudi Arabia. It could be the start of a bad, dare I say it, irritating joke. It wasn't, but it is funny how and where you come across people who appear in your life and help you to make sense of it.

We were there, not on some Saga style holiday – The Lawrence of Arabia package. We were there to speak at a major education technology conference. If I'm honest, whilst I knew of Steve and knew a little about his work, he was not the fellow speaker I was most looking forward to meeting. Now I have had the great privilege of meeting many amazing people in my life, but at this particular event, we both were going to have the opportunity to 'hang' with a man who has, arguably, changed the world: Steve Wozniak. Now when I say hang, what I mean is, grab two minutes to muscle in on a selfie with the great man. Imagine, by the way, my clear discomfort when I pulled a Samsung phone from my pocket for the snapshot moment.

I know that we were both looking forward to our 'Woz' moment but, I have to confess, it was an event and a circumstance that made me feel a little uncomfortable, as I felt a little like a fish out of water. This was an edtech event and I am not an edtech guy; just ask my kids. I am always a little intimidated around people who are experts at anything, but particularly people who know what buttons to press.

As a teacher, I remember the early days of edtech: BBC model B computers, tape recorders and vectorised maths games. I remember thinking at the time that this is all very nice but ...

Maybe those early encounters somewhat coloured my judgement, particularly when I started getting sent on courses run by my local authority, I was always the one sent because I was, at the time, the youngest member of staff in my primary school and, also, male! The courses were run by even younger, more thrusting guys, who spoke a language I had no understanding of; they were also able to play a keyboard like a virtuoso violinist. Like many, in those early days, I became a little dismissive, a defence mechanism I think.

Of course, over the following twenty-five years, tech became better, more user friendly and frankly, very groovy. I got into it and, as my confidence grew, so did my use of it as a teacher. Then things accelerated, because tech got cheap and the Internet transformed everything.

I have always had a big fear though, and that fear is this. I am an educator who truly believes that the moral imperative of what we do must be centred on the development of people; of individuals; their unique talents and interests and of their growing awareness of their own aspirations and values. For me, that is what education has always been and will always be about. What concerns me is that some people see technology as the answer to the future of education and, at times, I think that we have thrown huge amounts of money at that belief: filling classrooms with computers, then laptops and interactive whiteboards, palm tops and tablets …

I always worry when I am at an edtech event that people will get carried away with the latest flat screen, 4D, fibre optic portal and be seduced into believing that that is the holy grail. I passionately believe that technology is absolutely at the heart of life in the 21st century and can only imagine what it will do to the 22nd century, but I am also passionate that education is more than that, as is life. For me, technology can only be of power in the hands of educators who understand its context.

So it was that amongst the humps, rugs and wood smoke of that evening in Riyadh I made my tentative introduction to Steve Wheeler. As well as being a hugely impressive person and incredibly good company, he is also a skilled and passionate educator who sees the power of technology as a tool to support the education of our children; an education that is clearly about the development of gloriously organic, unpredictable beings. The next morning, we sat next to each other to hear Woz's address to the conference. It turns out that he too is deeply passionate about children and their future, it turns out that he has always been driven by the use of technology as a means to support the development of people and their lives, not as 'the answer'.

As I have got to know more about Steve, his work and this book, the more I have grown to admire a man who has the ability to communicate, in the most human of ways, how technology is a catalyst for the change so vital in our global education landscape. His work always returns to the power and potential of people; he is deeply human, accessible and provocative. He has taught me a great deal about the integration of education and technology and the future challenges we face. This is a fantastic book written by a hugely important figure in our education landscape. Whilst I will always have an image of that first meeting in my mind, if I'm honest, it is still the selfie with Woz which hangs on my office wall. This, however, is the book that will take pride of place on my shelf.

Introduction

They say that your school years are the best years of your life. For me, school was a strange place where lots of confusing things happened and very little made much sense. My formative years went by in a blur of indifference with the occasional memorable experience.

One such occasion was at the end of my time in school, when I met with my careers guidance teacher. This was 1972, during the heady days of the final lunar landings, where space exploration was top news. Space travel and moon landings had caught the imagination of just about every kid in the school. On a school trip the previous year I had also visited the Philips Evoluon, a science and technology exhibition run by the electronics manufacturer in Eindhoven, Holland. The building was shaped like a huge flying saucer. Inside, we had watched live science experiments and tried out exotic new technologies like video conferencing. It had fuelled my young imagination even more. The conversation with my careers guidance teacher went something like this:

'So, Wheeler, what do you want to do when you leave school next year?'

'I want to be an astronaut, sir.'

A moment's silence. A slight pause while the career teacher's spectacles glinted. He adjusted his tie, then ...

'Don't be silly, sonny. Being an astronaut isn't a real job.'

'Yes it is, sir.'

'No it isn't.'

'It's what I want to be, sir. I want to explore space and stuff.'

'Well, I'm afraid that's just impossible. Anyway, you have to be an American to be an astronaut.'

'Or a Russian, sir. They're called cosmonauts in Russia, sir.'

'Well, clearly you're neither, so you need to think again. What are you good at?'

This teacher works as a careers adviser at my school. He should know this, I thought. He should have done his homework on me.

'I'm good at art, sir.'

'Hmm. What else are you good at?'

'Music. Not a lot else.'

'OK ... not academic ... ' he muttered, jotting down a few notes, 'so you'll be an artist or a musician then. Good luck with that. Time's up, Wheeler, I have a lot of other students to see.'

He indicated toward the door, and I walked out, none the wiser.

And that, as they say, was that. I left school even more determined to be an astronaut, or more realistically, I resolved at the very least to get myself involved in some form of exploration. From my time studying geography and history, I had learnt about the explorers of old, including my heroes David Livingstone, Mungo Park (who always sounded to me like a municipal recreation area) and Robert Falcon Scott, whose mission to reach the South Pole ended in heroic failure.

Astronauts, I felt, were the last great explorers – launching into the deep unknown, exploring the final frontier – space. I wanted to boldly go where no one had been before. To be the first.

Captain Kirk and Mr Spock had a lot to answer for.

The years have flown by, and on reflection, somewhat indirectly, that is exactly what I think I have become – an explorer. I started my career as a graphic designer and photographer, then did technical work with videos and computers, before training as a psychologist. I was also a part-time musician, youth leader, a small businessman running my own independent record label, a lecturer in education, and finally a researcher and associate professor at a large university. In my mind this makes me an explorer, investigating previously unknown areas of education and discovering new forms of pedagogy. I experiment with social media and mobile technologies, learning how they can fit into new methods and contexts, trying them out to see what happens. My job is to navigate new and emerging theories and test their validity.

In a strange and roundabout way, I have actually fulfilled my schoolboy dreams to become an astronaut, although I now explore a different cosmos. This is the cosmos of the mind and technology. I explore learning in the digital age.

My convoluted journey has led me to the writing of this book. I wrote it by drawing on all my previous experiences and a diverse and eclectic range of skills and interests. I wanted it to focus on the big questions and major challenges that teachers face in the digital age.

So here it is. The book that is now open in front of you features my own personal stories and reflections about learning. It is an exploration of some of the new phenomena that I have noticed as a direct or indirect consequence of using technology in education. This book attempts to excavate the theory and practice of education in an age of disruption and change. It highlights new approaches to education in an era where technology is commonplace, and where mobile phones and social media are shaping the perceptions and behaviour of students. It is also a critique of the current education system.

Some of the sections in this book may seem familiar to regular readers of my blog 'Learning with 'e's'. That is because they started out as blog posts, and have subsequently been developed into a more considered and expansive commentary on pedagogy, technology and education. Some sections are presented as personal reflections and narratives, while others are based on empirical research.

Inevitably, this book also features some contributions from members of my personal learning network, teachers and other professionals who have contributed to the dialogue on my blog. It is inevitable because my personal learning network has had a profound influence on my thinking. To all of the wonderful educators who are featured, and to the many others who might have been if space had permitted, I value you and I thank you.

The commentary that runs throughout the book, although not exhaustive, will highlight many of the issues that are currently impacting upon teaching and learning in all sectors, including change and disruption, the redesign of learning spaces, the disputed nature of knowledge in the age of Google, and several new and emerging pedagogical explanations and theories. I pose some challenging questions about our changing identities, roles and positions in society as we teach and learn using digital technology. I point out some of the dangers of the digital age, such as the risk of technology becoming an obsession, and the issues of technophobia. We hear many stories of video game addiction, lost sleep due to excessive hours spent on social media, or relationship breakdowns due to compulsive use of the Internet.

I believe that for educators everywhere, the challenge is to take devices that have the potential for great distraction and boldly appropriate them as tools that can inspire learners, focus their minds, and engage them in learning.

I also propose the possibility that new technologies can provide solutions to some of the current problems of education. In an age where children seem to have a natural affinity with smartphones, computer games and social media, teachers face a big challenge – and a golden opportunity – to make a difference. This challenge is like no other. The challenge set before teachers and lecturers is to try to make sense of how new technology can promote learning, engage students and inspire them to sustain a lifelong career in learning.

In this book I cannot promise to provide any of the answers to the problems teachers currently face, but I will certainly pose some pertinent questions about the theory and practice of education. Hopefully, I will also offer hints to where some of the answers might be found, and how teachers can start to make a significant impact on the future of education.

So, if you're still with me, let's go on a voyage of discovery – to find out how the world of learning is changing, and how new technology – and you and I – can make a difference.

New Wine, New Wineskins

Every man is a creature of the age in which he lives, and few are able to raise themselves above the ideas of the time.

Voltaire

The search is on to discover the best ways technology can be used to enhance, enrich and extend learning. This is not an easy quest to achieve, because technologies do not sit easily alongside traditional pedagogical methods. And yet they should, because as Clay Shirky[1] argues, the social media tools and mobile phones we use are not alternatives to real life, they are now an integral part of it.

There should be no false distinctions between the real world and the digital world in schools. There are certainly none in the minds of students. Sadly, in institutional terms the distinctions do persist, because a notoriously conservative culture pervades schools and universities. New technologies and new ideas are regarded with suspicion. Computers are confined to 'special' labs in schools. Mobile phones are banned in many classrooms and social media services are blocked by education authorities. Video games are viewed as a distraction and a waste of time, and certainly nothing to do with learning.

Meanwhile, as education strives to preserve its old traditions, an entirely new generation of learners, immersed in the digital world from birth, is entering our gates. They are demanding – and expecting – new approaches to learning, approaches that incorporate technology.

---

1 Clay Shirky, *Cognitive Surplus: Creativity and Generosity in a Connected Age* (London: Penguin, 2010), p. 37.

All change

Incorporating new technology into everyday professional practice is not an easy prospect for the average teacher. Schooling in its present form was designed to meet the needs of a society that no longer exists. This is a view that is gaining a great deal of traction. In his famous TED Talk, Sir Ken Robinson[2] argues that while other professions are rapidly adapting to meet the changes, education is standing firm, stoically preserving its status quo. This is not simply rhetoric. It's a warning. The formal learning spaces, traditional approaches, standardised delivery of content, and the restrictive manner in which learning is measured, all seem increasingly anachronistic.

Society is in transition, and the changes are rapid and relentless. Organisations everywhere are investing in new technologies, and the world of work is constantly changing, shifting from centralised to disaggregated. Almost every week, news channels report the arrival of a new device or technology that will supposedly make our lives easier. The changes seem to accelerate, leaving us all just a little bewildered.

The futurist Ray Kurzweil[3] has suggested that where change was linear, now it is exponential. Change is now accelerating at an unprecedented rate. The result is that many traditional systems such as government, healthcare, transport, entertainment and communications are being disrupted and consequently transformed. Meanwhile, state-funded education stands like a rock amidst this maelstrom, largely unchanged.

---

2 Sir Ken Robinson, 'How Schools Kill Creativity', TED Talks (2006). Available online at: http://www.ted.com/talks/ken_robinson_says_schools_kill_creativity.
3 Ray Kurzweil, 'The Accelerating Power of Technology', TED Talks (2005). Available online at: https://www.ted.com/talks/ray_kurzweil_on_how_technology_will_transform_us.

Improving education

Is education changing at all? Some would assert that it is. Later in this book I will offer some evidence to support this claim. There are some signs in certain places that change is happening, but with change comes uncertainty and anxiety, and there is often a human price to pay. New technical infrastructures are now widely available, the Internet is familiar to many, and mobile devices are proliferating. This has prompted a rise in informal learning. The growth of movements such as Massive Open Online Courses[4] (MOOCs) are accelerating this growth, heralding an uncertain, turbulent future for formal education.

Clearly, those who are fighting to preserve what is good in education will need to ensure that what happens in schools and universities is relevant to this generation, and is reconciled with the needs of future society. However, they may be fighting a losing battle if they rely solely on technology. Simply introducing technology into the classroom is not enough. Teachers will need to understand how new technologies can be used to *improve* pedagogy. Additionally, education leaders will need to understand the link between change management and the optimisation of learning outcomes. Often this is less than explicit. Most crucially, all educators will need to know how pedagogy should change to meet students' needs in this disruptive era of technology and new working environments – teachers will need to understand the theory behind the practice.

Teachers will not achieve these quests by being timid, or reluctant to engage with technology. Nor, on the other hand, will they fully understand the benefits of technology if they believe that it is the *only* answer. Technology is not a silver bullet. Simply applying technology because it's new and shiny, or because 'everyone else is doing it', is almost always a mistake. It is a false economy, and it does children a disservice. It also opens the door for sceptics such as Larry Cuban[5] to argue scathingly that computers in schools are oversold and underused. Indeed, there is a truth to this opinion. Many schools and universities have cupboards full of technology

---

4   Fred G. Martin, 'Will Massive Open Online Courses Change How We Teach?' *Communications of the ACM* 55.8 (2012): 26–28.

5   Larry Cuban, *Oversold and Underused: Computers in the Classroom* (Cambridge MA: Harvard University Press, 2009).

that is gathering dust because no one actually figured out what to do with it before it was purchased. They are the proverbial solutions looking for problems to solve.

A greater problem arises when new technology is introduced into an old system only to be used to perpetuate old practices. Let me explain this with the help of an ancient tale.

An old story

We can learn a lot from old stories and ancient histories. This extract from the Bible illustrates the perennial problem:

> No man putteth new wine into old wineskins; else the new wine will burst the wineskins, and be spilled, and the wineskins shall perish. But new wine must be put into new wineskins; and both are preserved.
>
> **Luke 5:37–38**

This parable is often wrongly cited as 'new wine in old bottles'. To appreciate the full meaning of the metaphor, it's important to use 'wineskin' rather than 'bottle', so let's deconstruct the meaning behind the parable of the new wine in old wineskins.

Two thousand years ago in Israel, at the time of Jesus Christ and his disciples, wine was stored in skins. These were usually bladders fashioned from goat or sheep skin, which held the liquid. Invariably the wine would ferment inside the skins, forcing them to expand to their limit, eventually causing them to become brittle. Once used, the wineskins had to be discarded; otherwise, if reused, the new wine would ferment, expand them beyond their capacity, and cause them to burst. It was a false economy not to buy new wineskins to store the new wine. Wine was spoilt and money lost when the rubric was ignored.

The power of the parable therefore resides in the nature of the wineskin. It has been used to show how volatile it can be when old and new cultures collide. Alvin Toffler[6] illustrated this phenomenon in *Future Shock*, warning that where old and new cultures clash, there

---

6 Alvin Toffler, *Future Shock* (New York: Random House, 1990).

will be disorientation, confusion, stress, disruption … and there will also be winners and losers.

Disruption

Today we are witnessing a clash of cultures in education, across all the sectors of learning and teaching. In fact we have been facing this challenge for some time. It is a struggle between the old and the new, the closed and the open, the traditional and the radical. In this context, putting new wine into old wineskins means that new practices do not sit comfortably with old mindsets. I would develop this further to argue that it is difficult to explain or justify new methods with old theories. New approaches often break the boundaries and rules that were established by the old traditions, which results in a human cost. People become uncomfortable when their old practices are disrupted and they are forced to relinquish that with which they have become familiar. Some resist valiantly, others simply pay lip service.

Change is inevitable (except apparently, from a vending machine). Change is rarely an easy process to manage, and disruption is never fully welcomed by any profession, but it is not necessarily bad news. As well as presenting a threat, disruption can be a positive force, providing fresh opportunities to improve practice. The rapid influx of new technologies into formal education has already disrupted many old practices, and has created a fair amount of stress for practitioners who have become comfortable with old practices. But it has also ushered in new ways of doing things. There are winners and losers. Some teachers thrive, others merely survive, and some sadly fall by the wayside.

Change is exactly what educators face each and every day, but is it the right kind of change?

New wine technology

The parallels between the wineskin parable and the state of the current state education system are abundantly clear. A new society with new needs clearly requires new methods of teaching. I have heard it said that the 1.0 School is no longer able to effectively teach the 2.0 Student. Massified state-funded education is no longer adequate to support the needs of a distributed, diverse society. When what is offered does not meet the needs or satisfaction of students, they will either subvert the system or they will fail.

If a school bans mobile phones, the students will still use them anyway, most probably for unscholarly purposes. If new technology is used in the same way as old technology, the pedagogy 'wineskin' is likely to fail. If the new technology is used inappropriately we can expect a similar outcome. There is no pedagogy for irrelevance.

When interactive whiteboards (IWBs) were first introduced into classrooms, they were a surprise. After a short hiatus while the new tools were appraised, many teachers began either to overtly resist, or use them conservatively, often in the same way they had used the older dry-wipe whiteboards. This kind of ersatz compliance was in reality a passive form of resistance. Usually teachers resisted because of ignorance due to a lack of training, but it might also have been because of technophobia – a fear of the new technology and the discomfort it might bring. Again, the application of some useful pedagogical theory would have helped. An understanding of how interactive tools such as the IWB can be applied to engage students and to support their learning would transform its use in formal education.

There are alternative uses for the IWB which draw on pedagogical theories. Allowing children to come to the front to use the IWB would transform it from a didactic teaching resource into an interactive learning resource, and extend students' knowledge beyond what they could achieve on their own. Creating their own content on the IWB would increase their chances of developing a deeper understanding. However, teachers are often reluctant to allow students to touch the expensive equipment due to a host of perceived risk factors, or they simply don't conceive that student use might be possible – they see the IWB solely as a teaching resource.

And so the old practices continue, negating the disruptive, creative potential of the new technologies, with the result that teaching does not improve. Because teaching does not improve, learning does not improve. Teachers fail to capitalise on the affordances and potential of the 'new wine' technology, because they are still limiting their practice and imagination to the 'old wineskins' mindset of the past. This is a scenario that is played out time and again with the introduction of new technology into education. Ironically, it is not the technology schools introduce that will have the most impact on learning. The solution to the problem is staring us right in the face. The personal technology being brought into schools in the pockets of the students is going to be the real game changer.

Now that a large percentage of students in school own mobile phones, it is important that the old wineskin mentality of 'banning phones in class' should be discarded, and a new wineskin of 'let's discover together how we can harness the potential of smartphones in learning' should be applied.

New learning, new expectations

Technology is one issue. Pedagogy is another. The current generation of learners brings a new set of expectations to education. Sadly they are often thwarted by the old, outmoded models of teaching that persist in schools, colleges and universities. Inflexible delivery of teaching, outmoded assessment methods and siloed curricula do little to support the development of the Knowmad Society.[7] Knowmads, as John Moravec and his colleagues explain, are:

> Nomadic knowledge workers: creative, imaginative, and innovative people who can work with almost anybody, anytime and anywhere. The jobs associated with 21st century knowledge and innovation workers have become much less specific concerning task and place, but require more value generative applications of what they know. The office as we know it is gone. Schools and other learning spaces will follow next.

Clearly, Knowmads are a new breed of learners. They tend not to stay in one place for too long, and if the prediction above is correct,

---

7 John W. Moravec (ed.), *Knowmad Society* (Minneapolis: Education Futures, 2013). Available online at: http://www.knowmadsociety.com/download/.

they will not harbour any expectations about learning in one place. Most fundamentally, the manner in which they learn is different to the learning that characterises formal education. The Knowmad learns interactively, independently, autonomously. Whichever way we regard the future of education, many would accept that privileging teaching over learning is no longer tenable. Today's students need freedom to learn what, how, when and where they wish.

You will discover as you read this book that there is plenty of evidence to suggest that today's students are discovering new ways to learn, ways that are radically different to those of previous generations. They are more mobile, and more discerning about what is relevant to their personal lives and future plans. And although teachers generally recognise this, state-funded education has not advanced sufficiently or responded rapidly enough to support and nurture these new ways.

Often, in schools and universities, the new wine expectations are being let down by the old wineskins. Outside and beyond the walls of the school, society has new priorities that were unknown even a decade ago. These have arrived with such rapidity that they have caught the conservative, slow-to-change state education system off guard and ill-prepared to respond. The old wineskins are leaking at the seams, and are about to burst.

This is not simply rhetoric. Teachers are now preparing students for a world of work that has yet to be invented. It is not sensible, nor is it sustainable to continue to apply old methods. When students leave school and enter into that yet-to-be invented world, they will need to be equipped with a range of skills and literacies the preceding generation did not require. Not only will they need to be agile thinkers, they will also need to be able to solve problems that are exclusive to their generation, problems of which we are not yet aware. Some of the problems they will encounter may be uniquely caused by the very same future technologies they will use on a daily basis. Their ability to be flexible and responsive to change, and their skills of 'learning how to learn' will be just about all they have to help them survive. They will need to be digitally ready and technologically literate, probably beyond the experience and knowledge of their teachers and tutors.

As Singapore educator Craig Kemp observes, they will be the communicators, inventors and thinkers of the coming generation.[8] They will also discover, through their extensive and habitual use of online gaming, that the coding that sits behind the game can be modified to create new versions. This practice of 'modding' becomes, in Gee's terms,[9] a way to hack reality, borrowing from and modifying what already exists and using it to create something new. This is a practice that teachers can surely learn a lot from when it comes to developing new curricula or designing learning spaces.

These are not elements that feature in much of current formal education. Consequently, it may not be possible for students to learn these skills solely in school, college or university. They will discover new ways to learn these for themselves, leading to the conclusion that young people are already preparing themselves for work in the future.

It follows that if school is to contribute toward this development, teachers will need new pedagogies to support these new ways of learning while students are actually in school. This will mean radically changing the way education is conducted. It will also mean that new theories should be applied to explain and underpin the practices that will emerge to meet the new expectations and new ways of learning. We need new wineskins for new wine if we are going to save education. We need a new vision in our schools, colleges and universities to preserve that which is good and great about education – a wineskin that will cope with the vast, sweeping and fermenting changes that are about to engulf us.

---

8   Craig Kemp, 'What is School? Creating Change in Education.' Professional Reflection Blog (28 August 2014). Available online at: http://mrkempnz. com/2014/08/what-is-school-creating-change-in-education.html.
9   James Paul Gee, *What Video Games Have to Teach Us About Learning and Literacy* (New York: Palgrave Macmillan, 2003).

2
Changing Education

The greatest danger in times of turbulence is not the turbulence; it is to act with yesterday's logic.

Peter Drucker

In 1925, a family living in a backwoods, rural area of Virginia won a prize to visit New York City. They were a poor family, and lived in a small community, in a log cabin with no electricity. They drew their water from a well and most of their food was either traded or hunted for. And so the family dressed in their best clothes and travelled to the Big Apple by Greyhound bus.

They arrived in the centre of the large city, and emerged wide-eyed and confused in the middle of Times Square. They gazed up in wonder at the skyscrapers, and marvelled at the bustling crowd, the noise and the lights. They had never seen anything quite like it before, and couldn't believe there were that many people in the world.

After a few minutes, the woman said to her husband, 'Come on, let's go find Macy's.' Her husband asked, 'What is a Macy?' 'Macy's is a department store,' she explained, 'one of the biggest in the world. I've heard so much about it!' They walked a few blocks down Broadway with their two children and entered into the foyer of the huge department store. 'Come on, dear,' said the woman to her daughter, and off they went to see the ladies fashions.

The poor husband was left standing with his son, bewildered, in the middle of the large Macy's atrium. He saw hundreds of people milling around, walking up and down staircases, and then he noticed a queue forming over to one side. He wandered over to take a closer look.

He saw what appeared to be a door that slid open to let people into some kind of chamber. The door would then slide shut, and a dial above the door would rise and fall through a series of numbers.

When the door opened again, the people had changed. This happened several times, and the bemused man wondered what kind of strange machine this was in the wall, that could transform people before his eyes.

Then he watched as a little old lady with a walking stick hobbled slowly through the door. The door slid shut, the dial rose and fell, and the door slid open again. Out walked a beautiful, blonde bombshell of a woman. His jaw fell open in surprise.

He turned to his son, and said, 'Son, quickly – go get your mother!'

What are these strange machines?

Arthur C. Clarke once said: 'Any technology that is sufficiently advanced is indistinguishable from magic.' And therein lies a problem when we first try to introduce new technology into schools. We are seduced by it. It appears magical to us. We become enthusiastic about it to the point that it is seen as an answer to our problems, even though we don't know what the problem is yet. The trouble is, when we try to impress young people with these new technologies, we fail. What seems magical to us is probably nothing special to younger users, who have most likely seen it all before.

Learning in the digital age is different to any previous form of education. Teaching has always been a challenging profession, but in a time where technology is proliferating and has penetrated just about every aspect of our lives, teachers now have unprecedented opportunities to reform education and create previously inconceivable possibilities for learners. But they need to get past the idea that technology is special. It is not. Technology, just like any other set of tools, is there to help the user perform. In the case of learning technology, it fulfils the function of supporting learning. As such we should make it mundane. Technology that is transparent is more effective than technology that is so prominent that it demands our attention. Technology that frames learning so we can see 'through it' to engage and explore is more effective than technology that is the centre of attention. Introducing technology into schools is not difficult. Ensuring that it is used appropriately is another matter entirely.

Making a difference?

As we have seen, adapting to change is not easy, systems are slow to change, and new technologies are accompanied by their own unique problems. Not only must educators contend with huge demands on their time and energy, they now have to cope with rapidly changing environments while learning to use a bewildering array of emerging technologies. A prudent question to ask would be to what extent technology in schools has made any difference to teaching and learning.

A few years ago I was invited to sit on a discussion panel during a student teacher conference. Each of us was invited in turn to give a brief presentation on our teaching philosophy. As you would expect, my presentation heavily featured technology. Two of the other panellists challenged me to show how technology had made a difference in schools, as they were of the belief that it had made little impact. My response was concise – all I said was, 'Special Educational Needs'. My fellow panellists quickly conceded the point, because it is irrefutable. For many children, technology supports and enhances their learning, but for children with special needs, technology actually *enables* it to happen. Without adaptive technologies, children with hearing and visual impairment would be fully disadvantaged. If specialist software and technologies were not available, children with physical and cognitive disabilities would be disenfranchised, virtually excluded from mainstream education.

But it's not only special needs students who are benefitting from new technologies in the classroom – other students and their teachers are finding learning and teaching a more engaging prospect because of the affordances they offer. The relationship being forged between teachers and their students with technology is not a superficial one. UK teacher Drew Buddie recently stated: 'It's not about just shifting traditional lessons onto screens – it's about allowing pupils to make use of their devices to truly enhance their learning while giving teachers better ways to track individual achievement and personalise lessons.'[1]

---

1   Sophie Curtis, 'Digital Learning: How Technology is Reshaping Teaching'. *The Telegraph*, 23 August 2014. Available online at: http://www.telegraph.co.uk/technology/news/11051228/Digital-learning-how-technology-is-reshaping-teaching.html.

Technology has made a positive impact on the lives of millions of students and their teachers, making everyone's lives easier by transforming tedious and time consuming tasks into super-quick automated processes. However, it is sometimes a little more difficult to offer evidence that it has changed pedagogy for the better. Often, this is because teaching is a profession that has a long conservative history. Let me elaborate.

Many teachers start their careers with an idealistic perspective on education, and aspire to great things. Some simply talk about 'making a difference', while others want to 'contribute something important to society'. To some these may sound like the trite and naive comments heard during a beauty contest, but they are usually heartfelt sentiments that come from people who have somehow become inspired to carve out a career in the fraught, pressurised world of education. Teaching is often rewarding and challenging in equal measure. Those who stay within teaching for any considerable period of time are generally highly motivated to make that difference, aspiring to mould and develop young minds.

Sadly, many also leave the profession because they become disillusioned with the endless paperwork, behaviour management issues and huge workloads; in short, the culture of performativity in schools. They may enter into teaching newly qualified and idealistic about the changes they wish to make. Very quickly, however, they find that new ideas are not always welcomed, and that they are expected to comply with the methods and approaches the school advocates.

Those that stay learn some important truths about working in education. The first is that to survive, teachers need to learn as many shortcuts and time savers as they can. They need to be able to juggle several activities at once, multitasking continually to ensure that they reach the end of the day physically and mentally intact. Technology can help teachers to save time, but often it is restricted to 'teacher tools' such as email, software used to create resources, and technology that can be used to instruct.

Secondly, every successful teacher must also be a professional learner. The essence of good teaching is to get students to fall in love with learning. If teachers themselves aren't in love with learning, how can they possibly expect to succeed? The very best teachers are those who constantly update their own knowledge and skills, reflect on their practice, and view their work critically and objectively. The most innovative teachers are those who discover how to adapt to constant change; they become flexible and agile in their approach to education. When new challenges present themselves, the very best teachers view them as opportunities rather than threats.

Teaching is often challenging because it is a political battlefield. There are always battles to fight, and the curriculum is one particular area of dispute. Teachers are hard pressed to cover the curriculum during lessons, and because of the strict assessment regimes imposed in state schools, they often find themselves 'teaching to the test'. This is a topic I will return to in a later chapter. Teachers are also under increasing obligation to complete paperwork on an unprecedented scale. As Sir Ken Robinson[2] argued in his 2013 TED Talk, teaching is a creative profession where we should be able to take risks and innovate. Often this doesn't happen because there is simply not enough time, and teachers can also be risk averse, avoiding failure by maintaining the tried and tested methods. This is hardly an ideal context for promoting new, innovative approaches to education.

On the other hand, teaching is rewarding because we deal with the business of learning, both as educators and as professional learners. In teaching there are endless opportunities to make a real difference for individuals, their families, and for the wider community. In the grand scheme of things, teachers play a pivotal role in shaping the future lives of their students. Compared to all other professions, teaching is arguably the one that has the most profound, long term impact on our society.

Doctors save lives, teachers make lives.

---

2   Sir Ken Robinson, 'How to Escape Education's Death Valley', TED Talks (April 2013). Available online at: http://www.ted.com/talks/ken_robinson_how_to_escape_education_s_death_valley.

Shocks and stares

Most teachers will concede that they are members of a very demanding profession where it is often difficult to find time to keep up with the changes. It would be plausible to claim that we are living during the first time in education where teachers believe they know less about technology than their students. This can make teachers uneasy. Perceived lack of knowledge can be unsettling, especially for professionals.

There are other issues to contend with. Many working in education are worried about the impact of technology on their professional roles and identities. Some are so anxious they will do almost anything to avoid using technology, in or outside of school. Others are shocked by the rapid advance of technology and are left wondering where we are headed. Still others are concerned about the disruption technologies such as mobile phones bring to the classroom. Some overtly resist changes.

Through the ages, there has always been resistance to change. Specifically, there has always been opposition to new technologies. Sabotage – a word synonymous with subversion through deliberate destruction – was first coined in the 15th century following the attempts of Dutch workers to break the newly introduced and very unpopular textile looms. It was rumoured that the workers threw their wooden clogs, known as sabots, into the machinery to break the cogs, because they feared that the new machines would render human workers obsolete.

The same mentality was present when robots were introduced into the car manufacturing industry late in the last century, although less overt kinds of opposition manifested then. Even today, many people still shun the automated teller machines (ATMs) because they don't trust them, and would rather talk to a human teller or cashier.

The roots of technophobia

Why are some people averse to technology? Is it the shock of the new and a fear of the unfamiliar? Is it that people are simply resistant to change? Often it's the uncertainty that new technologies bring which seems to faze people into resisting them. Fear of the unknown has a strong effect on our thinking. Some of the warnings are on the surface, quite reasonable, but if you look just beneath the facade of the caveats, there resides a kind of techno-panic – an unreasonable fear of what the technology might really bring to society.

Much of our fear of technology is represented in popular culture. In movies such as *2001: A Space Odyssey*, *The Terminator* and *I, Robot*, our own creations become a threat to our future, our humanity, our very existence. This trope can be traced back to Mary Shelley's *Frankenstein*, and even farther back to the myth of Prometheus. Bizarrely, there are strong links from Mary Shelley (via her poet husband Percy Bysshe Shelley) to their family friend Lord Byron's daughter, the technophile Ada Byron (more commonly known as Ada Lovelace, acknowledged as a champion of early technology and the first computer programmer). Was there a connection between these two vastly opposing stances? We might surmise that the influences were there and that conversations between the Shelleys and the Byrons might have led to discussions around the social and moral implications of the emerging technology of the time.

This historical discourse has influenced the views of teachers. Some who were working in education when computers were first introduced were concerned about their future. Back in the eighties I recall one of my colleagues staring uneasily at the row of shiny new computers I had just installed. Eventually he plucked up the courage to voice his concern, asking me if I thought computers would one day replace teachers.

I referred him to the celebrated science fiction writer Arthur C. Clarke, who said: 'Any teacher who can be replaced by a computer, should be.'

Clarke's message was simple. Computers do not educate. They have no minds, possess no emotions and are not sentient. Computers, just like any other tool ever invented, are simply there to be used to leverage our physical strength, amplify our cognitive abilities and extend our potential. We will always need teachers, whatever changes technology brings. We would all be wise to avoid confusing the matter: teachers are there to educate, and technology is there to support the process.

Change and inertia

At the heart of this discourse is the understanding that education is desperately in need of reform. In *Creating Tomorrow's Schools Today*, author and former head teacher Richard Gerver[3] tackles these issues head on. He sees school as a very different place to real life. It is full of strange conventions and anachronistic devices that don't translate to the real world. A bell punctuates the passage of time, and a timetable dictates one's every move. People shuffle from room to room en masse.

School children, Gerver suggests, often feel that they leave real life outside the school gate; alienated in the artificial confines of the school. This is the education system we have fashioned for our children. This is schooling on an industrial scale. There is little scope for personalisation. Little has changed in schools, even though, ironically, the world of production and manufacturing has gone through radical transformation and is now but a vestige of its former self.

Technology may have been introduced into schools, but the pedagogy practised in many has resisted reform. The factory model of education persists, because in the mind of its proponents, it is still the most efficient, cost effective way to train the workforce of the future. The state-funded school is a system where one size must fit all, and where the individual is swallowed up in the machinery of the school day. It is the place where we entrust the future of our youth, the generation that will take our place. It is a system that was established for a bygone age, and the inertia inherent within this system ensures that little has changed for generations of learners.

---

3 Richard Gerver, *Creating Tomorrow's Schools Today* (London: Continuum Press, 2011).

The new machines

Educational technology has a short history. Networked technology was first introduced into schools several decades ago. Before this, teachers used display technologies, projectors, televisions and videos. Over time, the computer lab (or ICT suite) was established in many schools as a centre for learning with technology. It was a designated area where the use of computers could be centralised and controlled. The argument for this was that they were an expensive investment, and needed to be managed responsibly.

In truth, the history of the computer lab epitomises what schooling is all about. The manner in which all technology has been deployed in schools tends to perpetuate the control teachers hold over the learning process. It gives students little latitude for creativity, self-direction and exploration. In 1970, sociologist Alvin Toffler predicted:

> Within thirty years, the educational systems of the United States, and several Western European countries as well, will have broken decisively with the mass production pedagogy of the past, and will have advanced into an era of educational diversity based on the liberating power of the new machines.[4]

By new machines, Toffler meant computers and their associated tool sets. By mass pedagogy, he referred to the factory production model of education that schools have been caught in for over a century. More than four decades after Toffler's book was published, there is conflicting evidence that technology has actually delivered any significant improvement to pedagogy. For many schools technology brings very little change to the way teachers educate. The mass production pedagogy model stubbornly persists, and personalised learning seems far from the reach of many young people.

Outside of education, mobile phones have changed the way we communicate with each other, and social networking services such as Facebook have similarly transformed the way we conduct our relationships with our friends and family. Broadcast media are ubiquitous, with television received in just about every household on conventional TV sets, through our handheld devices, and even on large screens in the public areas of major cities around the world.

---

4   Alvin Toffler, *Future Shock* (New York: Random House, 1990).

Our leisure, health, economy and social lives have all been transformed by the impact of the World Wide Web, and many would agree we are a lot better off because of it. In fact, advances in interactive personalised technologies are so prominent that hardly a week goes by without some new innovation being trumpeted by the media.

Distractions

Other issues have distracted teachers from the widespread acceptance of new technologies. There is continuing concern over the safety of children on the Web and around mobile phone use. Horror stories abound in the media of children being exposed to pornography and other undesirable content, the dangers of contact with paedophiles, cyberbullying, sexting and other problems inherent with Internet use. Clearly these are issues of concern to those who are responsible for the protection of children. However, any response should be balanced against overreaction that actually negates opportunities for teachers to use technology to transform education. It is clear that technologies are neutral, and that the potential threats reside in society rather than in the technology itself.

The pedagogical opportunities these new tools afford, such as interactive touch surfaces on which children can experiment, create and manipulate images and text, have been largely ignored. Teachers are concerned about the damage of expensive equipment, and they worry about disruption to the traditional lesson. They are also acutely aware of their own lack of knowledge and fear having their ignorance exposed.

There is a plausible argument that the failure to adopt new practices arising from new technology provision can be blamed on a lack of good leadership. Occasionally this may be the result of lack of knowledge, but more often than not, it is a lack of time and resources that results in teachers failing to develop new pedagogies. This is where strategic leadership intervention could benefit the entire school. If teachers are not given additional time, nothing new can be expected.

Pockets of inspiration

Despite this, it's not all doom and gloom. Fortunately, some aspects of education *are* beginning to change. Governments in many countries are attempting a variety of reforms. Some are more successful than others, but ultimately change is slow, because change that is imposed from above is usually resisted. It is the change that is implemented from within the organisation that is the most effective and enduring.

There are pockets of inspiration and innovation, some of which will feature in later chapters. Slowly, new forms of learner-centred education are emerging as teachers across the globe attempt their own small reforms. The innovation we see in school classrooms today is often implemented by 'lone rangers'. These are visionary teachers, working alone with what they have, and exchanging their ideas and experiences with other kindred spirits via social media and within their local communities of practice.

What kind of new pedagogies are emerging as a result of technology provision in classrooms? Firstly, children are being encouraged to improve their writing and reading through the use of social media such as blogs and wikis. They are being encouraged to communicate more effectively through podcasts, videos and on social networking sites. A lot of creativity is being unleashed through the use of image sharing sites and touchscreen tablets, and new dimensions to learning are being realised through game playing.

Mobile learning takes the experience of discovery outside the classroom into the community the children will eventually work within. Interactive whiteboards, when in the hands of an innovative teacher, can enhance and enrich the entire learning encounter, with students becoming as actively involved in knowledge production as their teachers.

None of this can be achieved without some self-sacrifice by educators, some visionary leadership, some risk taking and no small amount of disruption. If these four elements are present, innovative pedagogical practices will begin to spread, and we will see a realisation of Toffler's prediction. If not, we will continue to be mired in mass production pedagogy.

Praxis makes perfect

There is an important concept at the heart of educational reform. It is one that should never change. Methods ebb and flow while theories and techniques fall in and out of favour, and yet through the years one thing should remain constant: at the heart of all good education is praxis.

Praxis is a word you will rarely hear mentioned in the staffroom or the faculty office. Even when it is mentioned, it is a poorly understood concept, and is not particularly well researched. And yet praxis is – or should be – right at the very heart of everything we do and who we are as educators.

So what is praxis? For educators, it is the nexus – the overlap – between theory and practice. Draw two intersecting circles, label them 'what I can do' and 'how I know', and praxis sits right there in the middle, in the overlap between the two. Praxis represents the sweet spot of education in action. It is the essence of what happens when theory is applied to practice, and it's essential for all deep learning. But there's a lot more to understand about praxis.

Oliver Quinlan, one of my former colleagues at Plymouth University, once wrote a very thoughtful blog post about praxis. He argued that the theoretical models we learn and the skills we acquire as teachers are inextricably entwined. They influence each other, and in effect, become a part of who you are, your identity as an educator:

> Your theoretical framework influences your practice, but your experience in the classroom also continues to shape your framework; the two are not separate.[5]

Others have also written eloquently about praxis. The Brazilian educator and theorist Paulo Freire defined the gaining of praxis as a means of escape from oppression and ignorance. He argued that one of the barriers to liberation is the 'oppressive reality that absorbs those within it' and suggests this lulls us into a false sense of security. The only way to counteract this, says Freire, is to get outside of it so we can then be in a position to take action against it.

---

5   Oliver Quinlan, 'Bringing Theory and Practice to Teaching' (2012). Available online at: http://www.oliverquinlan.com/blog/2012/10/23/praxis-bringing-theory-and-practice-to-teaching/.

This can be done only by means of the praxis: reflection and action upon the world in order to transform it.[6]

Freire is concerned here with liberty from oppression. This oppression takes the form of ignorance as much as it does chains, prison bars, or the walls of a ghetto. He is saying that praxis gives us the awareness, or consciousness, of where we are – a realisation of the predicament we are in. It is an awakening to our reality, and a call for action to do something about it. If we are in any predicament in education, it is that we are in need of radical change, but many of us don't know how to implement that change. Knowing, and then doing something based on the knowledge that there is a crisis, can be a powerful response. But it's a little more complex than that. Consider the following passage:

> We can now see the full quality of praxis. It is not simply action based on reflection. It is action which embodies certain qualities. These include a commitment to human well being and the search for truth, and respect for others. It is the action of people who are free, who are able to act for themselves. Moreover, praxis is always risky. It requires that a person 'makes a wise and prudent practical judgement about how to act in this situation'.[7]

Theory without action is just theory. It's hot air. Action without theory can be just as hollow. How can you justify your actions and decisions in the classroom if you have no theory to support you? How can you implement change in education when you are uncertain about the issues? The best equipped teachers are those who are best informed. The most effective way to understand theory is to test it out. The most successful teachers are those who not only innovate in their practice, but also know how to justify their actions through the application of appropriate theory. The most effective teachers are those who reflect on, in and through their practice to better understand how things can be improved.

Praxis pervades reflective practice and is the contextualisation of theory within action. It can, and should, always permeate every aspect of your professional practice and identity as an educator. It's time to stop thinking about theory and practice as separate concepts. The most innovative teachers find ways to meld the two together, so

---

6   Paulo Freire, *Pedagogy of the Oppressed* (London: Bloomsbury Publishing, 2000), p. 33.
7   Wilfred Carr and Stephen Kemmis, *Becoming Critical: Education, Knowledge and Action Research* (London: Routledge, 2003), p. 190.

that thinking and action – theory and practice – combine to enable us to create, develop and maintain the best possible learning environments for our students.

Digital praxis

Praxis extends even further than this. In an age of pervasive computing, social media and mobile phones, each of us has the capability to connect to a vast community of teachers and learning professionals around the world. With the right digital tools to hand, teachers can become *global* educators. Any educator can inspire good learning in remote parts of the world they would never physically be able to visit. We can reach into seemingly unreachable places where the right kinds of knowledge can literally make the difference between life and death. I will develop this theme in a later chapter.

Furthermore, we are in a time where students can participate in learning while on the move, tapping into discussions, content and tutor support from just about any location. Digital tools provide a number of previously unavailable affordances, which in turn open new doors to learning and new possibilities for education. Praxis in the digital age will involve teachers and students co-constructing new ways to teach and learn. They will not necessarily share the same physical space.

Praxis of the future will involve an entirely new culture of learning, where teacher and student negotiate their roles in the education process. Not only will digital praxis be the meeting place, the overlap for theory and practice, it will also represent and inform the blend of activities and roles, synchronous and asynchronous, local and remote, social and personal, the multi-literacies and multiple modes of learning that are now possible through technology.

Schooling or education?

Praxis is not the only word in education that is poorly understood. A lot of other words are tossed around in education without a full understanding of their meaning. The word 'education' itself is often associated with schooling, but to assume that the two are one and the same would be a serious error.

When Pink Floyd sang 'We don't need no education' what they really should have said was: 'We don't need no schooling' – (although this would not fit so neatly into the melody). Education, when experienced in its purest form, is liberating, mind-expanding, essential.

Often, schooling fails to offer this to children. For many the school experience is about uniformity, standardisation and synchronisation. Thomas and Seely Brown[8] call it the 'mechanistic approach' to education because it relies on systems of checks and repetition, and regards knowledge as something to be delivered, rather than something that can be discovered and negotiated.

In schools where the business of education is conducted as an industrial process, children are moulded to become compliant to authority, inculcated with the essential skills of reading, writing and numeracy, and then tested on their knowledge of the world around them. Children are batch processed by age, their behaviour is managed according to an approved formula, and little time is given for self-expression. Their performances are scrutinised, and testing provides the ultimate measure of their achievements. They are treated as though they are receptacles that receive knowledge. The teacher is employed to fill the receptacles, and as Freire[9] argues, the more meekly they allow themselves to be filled by this knowledge, the more highly they are regarded as students.

This is not education. It's indoctrination.

---

8 Douglas Thomas and John Seely Brown, *A New Culture of Learning: Cultivating the Imagination for a World of Constant Change* (CreateSpace, 2011).

9 Paulo Freire, *Pedagogy of the Oppressed* (London: Bloomsbury Publishing, 2000), p. 53.

Real education

Before we can understand how technology can enrich learning, we need to understand the ethos of education. So what is it really about? A closer examination of the origins of the word 'education' will reveal that it derives from the Latin word *educere*, which means to draw out, or to lead from within. What does this mean? If you are a teacher, you will know that you can either instruct from the front, or you can take a back seat by creating opportunities for your students to learn for themselves.

Many teachers switch between instruction and facilitation depending on the needs of the students and the context of the teaching. This is a choice each teacher has to make, but if they make the wrong decision there can be profound consequences. Getting in the way of learning can be just as much a problem as neglecting to support students. Swiss psychologist Jean Piaget once declared:

> Each time one prematurely teaches a child something he could have discovered for himself, that child is kept from inventing it and consequently from understanding it completely.[10]

To draw out learners from within and to bring out their very best, we must first accept that each has something within them to give. Undeniably, every child does have something unique to offer. Each has skills, abilities, knowledge, hopes, aspirations and personalities that can be nurtured and allowed to blossom. Teachers who ignore this will not only fail to draw out those individual attributes, they will also deprive children of a wonderful spectrum of opportunities to learn for themselves, and to learn how to learn.

Whether children are encouraged to learn for themselves or are directly instructed depends on each teacher's personal philosophy on education, and also the overarching ethos of the school. As a professional, does education for you mean schooling, or drawing out from within? Most teachers probably take the middle ground and oscillate between didactic delivery of content and the facilitation of learning. If they are honest, most teachers will admit they default to the instructional mode when they need to control behaviour, or

---

10 Jean Piaget, 'Piaget's Theory' in P. Mussen (ed.), *Carmichael's Manual of Child Psychology, Vol. 1* (Hoboken NJ: John Wiley & Sons, 1970), p. 715.

if they are simply required to 'get through' the content of a lesson. The curriculum can be a hard task master.

In its purest form, education is about drawing out the learner from within themselves, giving them space to express themselves, explore and play; to ask the 'what if?' questions and learn according to their own preferences and at their own pace. Generally, state-funded schooling cannot and will not provide the latitude for this kind of education to be realised. Friedrich Nietzsche is reported to have said:

> In large states public education will always be mediocre, for the same reason that in large kitchens the cooking is usually bad.

The best we can hope for within the present industrial school system is that each teacher will be agile enough to interpret what is imposed upon them in ways that offer children enough latitude to learn for themselves. A question all educators should ask is: are we keeping them within themselves, or are we drawing them out from within? The answer will be found in each teacher's personal philosophy, and the art of their pedagogy.

The Meaning of Pedagogy

If you ask someone to define pedagogy, they are likely to reply that it's about teaching children. One fairly limited definition of the word pedagogue is just that – a school teacher. Another, less kind definition suggests that pedagogues are people who instruct in a dogmatic or pedantic manner. We seem to have some constrained views on the nature of pedagogy and how it is conducted. To gain a clearer, more expansive understanding of pedagogy, we first need to examine the etymology, the origins of the word.

Like many other commonly used words in the English language, pedagogy has its roots in Ancient Greece. Affluent Greek families would have many servants (often slaves), one of whom would be specifically tasked to look after the children. Often these servants would lead or escort the children to a place of education. The Greek word for child (usually a boy) is *pais* (the stem of this is *'paid'*), and the word for leader is *agogus*; – thus a *paid-agogus,* or pedagogue, was literally a leader of children. Later, the word pedagogue became synonymous with the teaching of our young.

When seen in this context, we would probably all agree that pedagogy is about children's education. And yet this confines us to a very limited understanding of what pedagogy is, or has the potential to become.

If we accept the principle of 'leading or guiding someone to education' at face value then we are able to open up a whole new world of possibilities for learning. Teachers teach, but educators reach is an increasingly popular aphorism – and also a principle that is at the very heart of all true pedagogy.

True pedagogy is the antithesis of instructing from the front of the classroom. True pedagogy is leading people to a place where they can learn for themselves. It is drawing them out from within and encouraging them to harness their full potential. It is about creating environments and situations where people can freely express themselves, and hone the abilities and talents they already have. It is about supporting them as they create their own knowledge, interpret the world in their own unique ways, and ultimately realise their full potential as human beings. True pedagogy is not about absolutes, but is more likely to be about uncertainties. It has a wider implication than simply teaching children.

For me, and many other educators, good pedagogy is about guiding students of all ages to their learning. It's about posing challenges, asking the right questions at the right time, and presenting relevant problems for learners to explore, answer and solve. It is being constantly vigilant for that 'teachable moment' which students will never forget.

Pedagogy in the digital age is profoundly social, involving the negotiation of meaning and the co-construction of knowledge. It is about learning together. True pedagogy is where educators transport their students to a place where they will be amazed by the wonders of the world they live within.

As Socrates once said, 'Wisdom begins in wonder.'

3

Theories for the Digital Age

He who loves practice without theory is like the sailor who boards a ship without a rudder and compass and never knows where he may cast.

Leonardo da Vinci

Learning today

Learning in the industrialised society is now acted out in front of a largely technological backdrop, where the use of digital media is assuming increasing importance. The present technology-rich learning ecology is characterised by the sustained use of digital media, its integration into formal contexts, and a shift towards personalisation of learning. As we have already seen, personal mobile devices, social media and easy access to the Internet are changing the learning landscape. Students are creating as well as consuming content, and user-generated content is proliferating across the Web. This is a feature that characterises learning with social media in informal settings. In formal settings too, students are taking greater responsibility for their own learning, creating their own learning and discussion spaces online outside of the auspices of the parent institution. They are engaged in unprecedented levels of peer learning, supporting each other through a variety of new technologies and personal tools.

The kind of learning described here is largely informal, outside the traditional education environment, transgressing the boundaries set by organisations. Informal learning is generally location independent, a topic that is elaborated upon in a later chapter. These facets of contemporary learning, when seen holistically, have led some educators to question the validity of pre-digital age learning theories. Consequently, in recent years several new explanatory theories have been proposed as lenses to critically view, analyse and problematise emerging forms of learning. Before embarking on any form of educational practice, teachers will benefit from an understanding of pedagogical theory.

In theory

There are at least two reasons why theory is important. Firstly, theories help us to explain what we are seeing or experiencing from a particular perspective. Theories frame our reality. Secondly, theories can inform and justify our professional practice as teachers.

The longer teachers work in education, the more they realise that there are many theories of learning. Although new and emerging theories are useful, especially in helping us to frame strange and unfamiliar learning scenarios, it would be foolish to ignore the older learning theories. In this book I will therefore reconsider some of the social and psychological theories of learning that many teachers are already familiar with. We need the best of both worlds. True digital praxis concerns itself with, and seeks to explain, learning that occurs in contexts and environments that previously did not exist.

Most of the older theories of pedagogy were formulated prior to the introduction of digital technology. They are useful for explaining what education has been in the past, and have also be used to frame what we see today in schools and universities. But in a technology-rich world where education is changing, some might question whether they are still adequate and relevant, or whether they need to be replaced or revised. As professional practitioners, we should certainly question whether older theories are still useful, but we should also ask whether the newer theories add anything significant to our understanding of learning in new digital contexts.

New theories, new questions

Some new and emerging learning theories do appear to offer fresh insights into learning in the digital age. Some useful new explanatory frameworks are directly related to technology supported learning, including heutagogy, which describes a self-regulated approach to learning; paragogy, a new model of peer to peer learning; a postmodernist explanation using the metaphor of rhizomes; and a distributed learning theory known as connectivism.

Might it now be time for these new theories to replace the old ones? Are the old theories still adequate to describe the new forms of learning that we witness today in our hyper-connected world? Do older theories miss some of the more subtle nuances of technology supported learning, or can they work together with the new theories to provide us with a basis to understand what is happening?

How can we, for example, explain learning activities such as blogging, social networking, crowd-sourced learning, or user-generated content such as Wikipedia and YouTube, using older theories? How might we begin to understand the issues surrounding folksonomies, peer learning, the wisdom of crowds, or collaborative informal learning – which seem to occur spontaneously, outside the classroom, spanning the entire globe – using old theories that were written to describe what happens in a classroom?

The questions above are deliberately provocative, but this is a discussion teachers need to have. Which models and theories should we use to explain learning through technology? In this chapter we will explore some of these emerging theories and evaluate them in the context of new learning cultures.

Connectivism

Our view of knowledge is changing. Some would argue that knowledge never changes, but today it is more highly interconnected than ever. Increasingly in this digital age so are people, and we now see knowledge being negotiated within communities and across networks at a global level. Knowledge is represented in new and previously inconceivable ways within self-organised spaces – and has never been so plentiful and diverse. It has also never been so volatile and open to change. Everyone, it seems, can add to knowledge at any time, using the devices in their pockets.

Our understanding of our world is changing rapidly as a result of our connections, to others and to content through vast networks and widely distributed computational power. Learning is changing because of these connections, prompting research into its influence on our minds, how it is changing knowledge and how it is advancing our understanding of learning processes.

One emerging school of thought that attempts to explain these phenomena is a new representation of learning known as Connectivism. Initially proposed by George Siemens,[1] Connectivism has been lauded as a 'learning theory for the digital age', because it seeks to describe how students who use personalised, online and collaborative tools learn in different ways to those of previous generations.

One of the tenets of Connectivist theory is that learning is lifelong, largely informal, and that previously human-led pedagogical activities and processes can be offloaded onto technology. Arguably, the third of these tenets is the most revolutionary. It derives from dissatisfaction with existing learning theories.

In his writings, Siemens criticises the three most dominant learning theories, namely behaviourism, cognitivism, and constructivism, and argues that they all locate learning inside the learner. His counter proposal is that through the use of networked technologies, learning can now be distributed *outside* the learner, within personal learning communities, through computer connections and across social networks.

Perhaps the most significant contribution Connectivist theory has made is the premise that declarative knowledge can now be supplemented or even supplanted by an alternative to memorisation. Knowing *where* knowledge can be found is a significant advance on simply knowing about something. In a nutshell, Connectivism holds that digital media has enabled knowledge to be distributed wider than ever, and what is now important is that students know where to

---

1   George Siemens, *Connectivism* (2002). Available online at: http://www. elearnspace.org/.

find the knowledge they require, rather than personally internalising it.

Knowledge now resides in the network and on devices as well as in people. This is a significant departure from previous theories where knowledge is always located within the individual. Connectivism thus defines knowledge in a new way: as mutable, distributed and shared across networks.

Connectivism places the onus firmly upon individual students to develop their own personalised learning tools, environments, learning networks and communities, where they can 'store their knowledge'.[2] Interestingly, this aligns neatly with the views expressed by a Canadian media theorist several decades before the Web blinked into existence. In the view of Marshall McLuhan, as we embrace technology 'our central nervous system is technologically extended to involve us in the whole of mankind and to incorporate the whole of mankind in us.'[3]

Time will tell how intimately we will connect with our technologies, but the mere fact that many of us are 'always on' is a key indicator to where and how we discover new knowledge.

Self regulated learning

Informal and self-regulated learning are defining characteristics of contemporary learning. Various commentators suggest that as much as 70 per cent of learning occurs outside of formal educational settings.[4] If these are accurate claims, they present a significant challenge to schools, colleges and universities. One decision education providers must make is whether they will respond to the desires of students to self-regulate their learning activities through personal technologies.

This presents a significant challenge. Institutions that do not support the Bring Your Own Device (BYOD) movement may be seen by their students as behind the times. Those who do support BYOD

---

2   Ibid.

3   Marshall McLuhan, *Understanding Media: The Extensions of Man* (Chicago: MIT Press, 1994), p. 4.

4   Jay Cross, *Informal Learning* (Hoboken NJ: John Wiley & Sons, 2006).

for students will need to invest significant time and resources into ensuring cross-platform operability and seamless delivery to students' personal technologies.

Self-regulation of learning is an important characteristic of personalised learning[5] but can also be seen within social learning environments. A number of collaborative and social networking services regularly play a role within the average student's personal learning environments, managed through their personal technologies. Self-regulation has been shown to enhance and improve learning outcomes,[6][7] enabling learners to achieve their full potential.[8]

Personal technologies enable self-regulation at a number of levels, including the 'object' and 'meta' levels of learning, supporting maintenance, adaptation, monitoring and control of a variety of higher level cognitive processes.[9]

By using personal devices as mind tools to offload simple cognitive tasks,[10] students can extend their own memories, build their confidence, and increase their motivation levels.[11] Furthermore, personal technology enables individuals to gain access to and participate at many levels within their communities of practice, from 'entering by learning' through to 'transcending by developing'.[12]

5   Jos Beishuizen, 'Does a Community of Learners Foster Self-Regulated Learning?' *Technology, Pedagogy and Education* 17.3 (2008): 183–193.

6   Scott G. Paris, James P. Byrnes, and Alison H. Paris, 'Constructing Theories, Identities, and Actions of Self-Regulated Learners', *Self-Regulated Learning and Academic Achievement: Theoretical Perspectives* 2 (2001): 253–287.

7   Karl Steffens, 'Technology Enhanced Learning Environments for Self-Regulated Learning: A Framework for Research', *Technology, Pedagogy and Education* 17.3 (2008): 221–232.

8   Manuela Delfino, Giuliana Dettori and Donatella Persico, 'Self-Regulated Learning in Virtual Communities', *Technology, Pedagogy and Education* 17.3 (2008): 195–205.

9   Thomas Nelson and Louis Narens, 'Metamemory: A Theoretical Framework and New Findings', in G. H. Bower (ed.), *The Psychology of Learning and Motivation* (New York: Academic Press, 1990): 125–141.

10 David H. Jonassen, *Computers in the Classroom: Mindtools for Critical Thinking* (Englewood Cliffs NJ: Prentice-Hall, 1996).

11 Sandra Goldsworthy, Nancy Lawrence and William Goodman, 'The Use of Personal Digital Assistants at the Point of Care in an Undergraduate Nursing Program', *Computers Informatics Nursing* 24.3 (2006): 138–143.

12 Thomas Ryberg and Ellen Christiansen, 'Community and Social Network Sites as Technology Enhanced Learning Environments', *Technology, Pedagogy and Education* 17 (3) (2008): 207–220.

Today all of this can be achieved by students beyond the formal surroundings of school or university, with no time or location constraints.

Heutagogy and MOOCs

There is a sense that personal technologies encourage learners to become more self-determined in their approach to education. Hase and Kenyon's conceptualisation of self-determined learning, which they call heutagogy,[13] places the emphasis on non-linear, self-directed forms of learning, and embraces both formal and informal education contexts.

The central tenet of heutagogy is that people inherently know how to learn. The role of formal education is to enable them to confidently develop these skills, encouraging them to critically evaluate and interpret their own personal reality according to their own personal skills and competencies.

The ethos of heutagogy extends to learner choice, where students can create their own programmes of study, a feature often seen in the loose and unstructured aspects of some of the earlier Massive Open Online Courses (MOOCs). The cMOOCs – those organised around the principles of connectivism – were created so that learners could join informal online learning communities, participate on their own terms, learn at their own pace, and even choose their own modes of assessment. Learning in cMOOCs is democratic, largely self-governed and premised on self-determined needs and outcomes.

Ultimately, heutagogy is aligned to other digital age theories, in that it places an importance on meta-learning or 'learning to learn', and also privileges the sharing and repurposing rather than hoarding of that knowledge. There are no limitations to the free dissemination of knowledge, and it is clear that this can be facilitated with ease through the use of social media and personal devices.

---

13 Stewart Hase and Chris Kenyon, 'Heutagogy: A Child of Complexity Theory', *Complicity: An International Journal of Complexity and Education* 4.1 (2007).

Paragogy

Another notable characteristic of digital age learning is peer learning. Highlighting the fast paced nature of the Web, Thomas and Seely Brown[14] suggest that peer learning can be both timely and transient. They show that never before has access to information and people been so easy and so widespread, and that we make connections with people who can help us manage, organise, disseminate and make sense of the resources.

Such interconnectedness and willingness to share within a community creates a new kind of peer mentoring that operates at multiple levels and many degrees of expertise, supporting learning in all its complexity.

Corneli and Danoff's notion of Paragogy[15] relates to the peer production of learning and depicts learners as co-constructors of their own learning, but as Corneli[16] warns, such an agenda may be at odds with established educational systems in some respects, and may even be opposed by others. This is due to the challenge that 'students teaching themselves' might pose to the privileged knowledge and power structures many formal educational institutions continue to hold so dear.

In essence, the Paragogy thesis is based on the argument that online environments are now sufficiently developed to support peer production of content which can be shared freely and widely, and can promote learning for all within any given community. Again, this echoes the Connectivist and Heutagogical ideals discussed earlier in this chapter, whilst at the same time presenting a challenge in terms of the quality, reliability and provenance of content.

These are not trivial issues. The user-generated content currently available on the Web has been criticised for its inconsistent quality[17] and its potential to encourage plagiarism, piracy and a host of other

---

14 Douglas Thomas and John Seely Brown, *A New Culture of Learning: Cultivating the Imagination for a World of Constant Change* (CreateSpace, 2011).

15 Joseph Corneli and Charles Jeffrey Danoff, 'Paragogy', OKCon (2011).

16 Joseph Corneli, 'Paragogical Praxis', *e-Learning and Digital Media* 9.3 (2012): 267–272.

17 Nicholas Carr, *The Shallows: What the Internet is Doing to Our Brains* (New York: W. W. Norton & Company, 2011).

nefarious practices.[18] User-generated content has also attracted criticism over issues of mediocrity, lack of accuracy and superficial scholarship.[19] [20]

Notwithstanding, many are now turning to Web-based user-generated content to educate themselves and to share their learning. In many ways, this is not simply a convenient option. The ability to use personal technologies to create, organise, share and repurpose content, in a diverse variety of formats with such ease across the global Web has become a democratising, liberating factor in education.

There are now many new ways students can create peer networks, learn from each other and share their ideas. In so doing, they are building what Ivan Illich[21] once termed 'the learning webs' that can enable every participant to define themselves by learning from, and contributing toward, the learning of others.

A postmodernist perspective

Postmodernist views of society can also be appropriated as lenses to analyse the use of personal devices in learning and the wider impact of technology on society. The rejection of structures and hierarchies that feature so prominently in postmodern theories is reflected in the common everyday uses of the Internet.

Consumers of Web-based content tend to search randomly and nomadically, because of the multi-layered, multi-directional capability of hyperlinked media. These seemingly random and digressive behaviours actually align quite conveniently with certain postmodern theories. Deleuze and Guattari,[22] for example, feature the nomadic thought processes that characterise contemporary perceptions, and portray the chaos of modern life. Their 1980

---

18 Andrew Keen, *The Cult of the Amateur* (New York: Doubleday, 2007).

19 Tara Brabazon, *The University of Google: Education in the (Post) Information Age* (Aldershot: Ashgate Publishing Ltd, 2012).

20 Tara Brabazon, *Digital Hemlock* (Sydney: University of New South Wales Press, 2002).

21 Ivan Illich, *Deschooling Society* (London: Penguin, 1971).

22 Gilles Deleuze and Félix Guattari, *A Thousand Plateaus: Capitalism and Schizophrenia* (London: Bloomsbury Publishing, 1988).

publication *A Thousand Plateaus* was hailed by some as a masterpiece of postmodernist writing. Others criticised it for its dense, pseudo-scientific prose.

Whatever the verdict, it was notable for introducing rhizome theory as a metaphor for knowledge representation. According to Deleuze and Guattari, rhizomes are unlike any other kind of root system, having no centre and no end. Rhizomes don't follow the rules of normal root systems, because they resist organisational structure and chronology, 'favouring a nomadic system of growth and propagation'. In plain English, the authors are attempting to describe the way ideas spread out naturally to occupy spaces just like water finds its level. They argue that the rhizome is not linear but planar, and can therefore spread out in any and all directions, connecting with other systems as it goes.

The same might be said about the way learning communities form, create their preferred ways of communication and decide upon their priorities. Deleuze and Guattari further employ the botanic metaphor of rhizomatic root systems to describe multiple, chaotic, non-hierarchical constructions of knowledge. Rhizomes resist chronology and organisational structures, and in doing so, more accurately represent the unstructured and chaotic but ultimately purposeful manner in which many people now use the Web.

Significantly, because rhizomes are open ended, the importance of Deleuze and Guattari's rhizome explanation is not invested in individual components, but rather in the direction and speed of motion the entire organism can adopt at any given time. This is reminiscent of self-organising spaces on the participatory Web, which consist not so much of the insights and offerings of individuals, but rather of what James Surowiecki[23] has termed 'the wisdom of the crowds'.

Crowd wisdom is evidenced in the seemingly random folksonomic directions chosen by entire communities of users as having meaning and importance. The community decides what is important to learn, so in effect, the community becomes the curriculum.

---

23 James Surowiecki, *The Wisdom of Crowds: Why the Many are Smarter than the Few and How Collective Wisdom Shapes Business, Economies, Societies and Nations* (New York: Abacus, 2010).

Rhizomatic learning in digital environments

A prominent contributor to the development of rhizomatic learning theory is Canadian teacher Dave Cormier. He takes this concept deeper into digital territory by equating rhizomatic learning with 'community as curriculum'. The advent of social media, mobile communications and digital media facilitate large, unbounded personal learning networks that mimic the characteristics of rhizomes. If we accept that there is a need for a living curriculum, it would be logical to also accept that a self-determined community generates and negotiates its own knowledge, thereby forming the basis of what its members learn.

Rhizomatic learning is also premised on an extension of community as curriculum, where 'knowledge can only be negotiated, and the contextual, collaborative learning experience shared by Constructivist and Connectivist pedagogies is a social as well as a personal knowledge–creation process with mutable goals and constantly negotiated premises.'[24]

For Cormier a rhizomatic interpretation of education is useful because it embraces the ever changing nature of knowledge. It is open ended, and is not driven by specific curricula – learning is constructed and negotiated in real time by the contributions of those engaged in the learning process'. It is useful to describe self-organised digital spaces where people store knowledge and connect with each other.

---

24 David Cormier, 'Rhizomatic Education: Community as Curriculum' (2008). Available online at: http://davecormier.com/edblog/2008/06/03/rhizomatic-education-community-as-curriculum/.

Wikipedia and self-organised learning spaces

According to Manuel Lima[25] Wikipedia is one of the largest rhizomatic structures ever created. The online encyclopaedia site has enjoyed meteoric success because anyone can contribute and edit content. Due to the open nature of Wikipedia and the highly connected nature of knowledge, contributors to the site are creating and organising their content in increasingly sophisticated and complex layers. Key words are connected through hyperlinks and there appears to be no particular limit or boundary to the layers and interconnections that are created. More pages are added each day about a myriad of topics. It's a work that will never be completed.

Clay Shirky[26] points out that Wikipedia articles become more accurate over time, because older errors are corrected more quickly than new errors can be introduced. Content that is good remains whilst content that is inaccurate or erroneous is eventually removed. It is a living, evolving repository of knowledge. This process leading to the survival of the fittest content has been described as Darwikianism.[27]

This kind of negotiated meaning through crowd-sourced reiteration is also recognisable in the knowledge-making processes that occur within the transient discussion threads and ephemeral collaborative spaces elsewhere on the World Wide Web; plus it can be observed in the open source movement and in the use of Creative Commons licensing, which supports the free sharing and repurposing of digital content.

The colonisation and navigation of knowledge spaces by communities is also self-sustaining. In Deleuze and Guattari's terms, we see individuals enacting nomadic roles and adopting a constant state of becoming. Again, this is reminiscent of the random searching,

---

25 Manuel Lima, 'Royal Society of Arts Animate: The Power of Networks' (2012). Available online at: https://www.youtube.com/watch?v=nJmGrNdJ5Gw.

26 Clay Shirky, *Here Comes Everybody: The Power of Organizing without Organizations* (London: Penguin, 2008), p. 119.

27 Steve Wheeler, 'Using Wikis in Teacher Education' in M. Lee and C. McLoughlin (eds.) *Web 2.0-Based e-Learning: Applying Social Informatics for Tertiary Teaching* (Sydney: IGI Global, 2011), p. 180.

scanning and jumping around content through hyperlinking that learners participate in as they traverse the digital landscape.

In effect, students participate as *flâneurs*, acting as individual agents, investigators and explorers of their own personal digital terrains. Their seemingly aimless behaviour, says Baudelaire,[28] 'belies their essentially purposeful wandering, as learners interrogate their environment in attempts to make sense of it, understand it, participate in it, and ultimately portray it to others'.

Rhizome theory is also a useful framework for understanding self-determined learning – the heutagogy described by Hase and Kenyon.[29] Hase and Kenyon place heutagogy in the frame of complexity theory, and suggest a number of characteristics, including 'recognition of the emergent nature of learning' and 'the need for a living curriculum'.

The self-determined pathway to learning is fast becoming familiar to learners in the digital age, and is also the antithesis of the formal, structured learning found in traditional education.

Endnote

One problem with the new theories is that they are often descriptive of specific new phenomena. Although currently chaotic, networked and digitally mediated communication and learning is widespread, it could also be a transient phenomenon. Further evolution of technologies and increased reliance upon their use in human activities may advance society into completely new, unexpected and unpredictable directions. We may then be in a similar position, seeking yet more theories to describe new activities. The measure of a good theory is whether it stands the test of time and continues to provide adequate, generalisable explanations.

The chapter that follows examines older, more established pedagogical theories and applies them within new, technology-supported learning contexts.

---

28 Charles Baudelaire, *The Painter of Modern Life and Other Essays* (New York: Da Capo Press, 1964).
29 Stewart Hase and Chris Kenyon, 'Heutagogy: A Child of Complexity Theory', *Complicity: An International Journal of Complexity and Education* 4.1 (2007).

4
Old Theories, New Contexts

If the facts don't fit the theory, change the facts.

Albert Einstein

As we become more acutely aware that our world is changing, we also realise that the change is accelerating. This is largely due to the proliferation of technology in recent years and the exponential effects it exerts on society. Technology not only provokes change, it also makes us more aware of that change.

Setting aside the less welcome effects of rapid change, technology seems to be having some positive influences on education. Knowledge is being democratised because learning is becoming more participatory and collaborative. Open access and open licensing provide increasing access to diverse content and as we have seen, new learning opportunities are being created every day, often by the learners themselves. Indeed, user-generated content is one of the defining features of the participatory Web.

Where once experts had a monopoly on knowledge and expertise, now anyone, it seems, can access content they can learn from. Autodidacticism – the act of self-teaching – is on the rise.

Vygotsky and learning

You can now teach yourself with technology. This is quite a departure from most traditional models of education. According to Lev Vygotsky, a very respected Russian psychologist of the last century, learning on your own is not as powerful or extensive as learning alongside a 'knowledgeable other' person. That person would normally be a teacher, but they could also be a peer, older sibling or parent. According to his Zone of Proximal Development theory (ZPD), children learn more extensively and richly within a social context, and learning is extended and accelerated through dialogue with the knowledgeable other person.

ZPD theory ran counter to other developmental theories of the time. Swiss psychologist Jean Piaget, for example, famously claimed that children were solo-scientists, exploring the world and constructing meaning for themselves through their direct interaction with their environments. He believed they would need to progress through a strictly defined set of cognitive stages before they were ready to learn at the next level.

Vygotsky's view of learning was laced with rich social contexts and laden with cultural nuances, and he didn't hold to stage development theory as strictly as Piaget. Like Piaget, Vygotsky subscribed to the notion that we construct our own meaning, but he believed that what you can learn on your own is limited when compared to what you can learn with someone else in close proximity, supporting and encouraging you. In other words, indirect learning, filtered by a knowledgeable other person, is a powerful thing.

American psychologist Jerome Bruner developed this concept a little further, describing how learning can be scaffolded. He believed that close support should be offered to students as they developed their skills, knowledge and expertise, and then, as they became more independent, the scaffolding could be gradually faded and eventually removed.

Self-organised learning

At the Glasgow Commonwealth Games of 2014, the winner of the men's javelin competition was Julius Kiplangat Yego. Representing Kenya, Yego's gold-medal-winning throw was measured at 83.87 metres. The secret of his success? He learnt how to throw the javelin by watching YouTube videos.

Today, we can boldly claim that anyone can learn just about anything they wish, because social media channels provide the content. Choose any subject, whether it be baking a sponge cake, playing blues guitar, or learning the art of animal husbandry, and you will find dozens of YouTube videos that will teach you. The content is out there somewhere. All you need to do is find it, and then make the commitment to learn through hours of practice and application.

In Vygotskiian terms, the knowledgeable other (the social context) is largely replaced by the technology. Vygotsky might not easily concede this point though. He might argue that behind the technology are the experts. They create the content and present it to you on YouTube, and the ZPD is still there. In effect, the technology is now mediating the social interaction between the learner and the knowledgeable other person.

Conversely, in Piagetian terms it could be argued that, in fact, the learner is still a solo explorer, discovering for himself that eventually he can, with a lot of practice and a great deal of trial and error, bake the perfect sponge cake, emulate Eric Clapton's finest blues riffs, or run a successful sheep farm in the hills of Cumbria. Great content is available on just about any subject in the curriculum via YouTube. Teachers everywhere are creating innovative videos and posting them for free use. One of the most innovative sets of videos I have seen is the History Teachers series created by Hawaiian educators Amy Burvall and Herb Mahelona. They take well-known pop songs and revise the words to represent vivid moments in history through music, animation and drama.[1] Mahelona is amazed at the reach and impact of the videos. He says:

> I am still wrapping my head around the idea that people all over the world are watching the videos we created for our classes. We are here on these little islands in the middle of the Pacific, and I think it's a testament to the value and educational validity of technology when something we create here can be instantly accessible and effective in another classroom in another part of the world.[2]

From a Vygotskiian perspective this technology becomes the knowledgeable other in the ZPD as it mediates the learning process. Implicit in video is the social support, the scaffolding. From a Piagetian perspective, the technology is simply another part of the environment, a set of tools that enable the construction of new

---

1 Amy Burvall, YouTube History Teachers Channel, 2013. Available online at: https://www.youtube.com/user/historyteachers.
2 Stuart Huggett, 'Learning to Rewrite History', *SQ Magazine*, 9 September, 2011. Available online at: http://sqmagazine.co.uk/2011/09/feature-learning-to-rewrite-history/.

learning. The learner is still a solo explorer, discovering for themselves, through trial and error, what is possible.

Which is the correct perspective? It's open to discussion, but whichever way we look at it, tools such as YouTube are opening up unprecedented and very rich learning opportunities for anyone who has access to the Web.

It's no surprise that informal learning is growing in popularity.

Freire and blogging

In my view, one of the most powerful ways of using social media for informal learning is blogging. The great Brazilian educational thinker Paulo Freire died in 1997, just as the World Wide Web was beginning to emerge in the Western, industrialised world. Sadly, Freire didn't live to see the powerful influence of social media on learning, or the impact blogging would have on education. We can only speculate on what he might have said about blogs if he had been witness to the participatory Web in all its present glory.

What follows is my interpretation of some of his ideas drawn from his most celebrated book, *Pedagogy of the Oppressed*, presented in six key points as they might be applied to the experience of educational blogging.

1. Respond to reader comments with humility. Freire wrote: 'Dialogue cannot exist without humility. Dialogue, as the encounter of those addressed to the common task of learning … is broken if the parties (or one of them) lack humility. How can I dialogue if I always project ignorance onto others and never perceive my own?'[3]

    This is not just a message for educational bloggers. It is a message for teachers everywhere. How can we stand there in a self-proclaimed position of enlightenment and view our students (or audience) as being in a state of ignorance? This is hubris of the first order. And yet that is what happens in many classrooms across the world every day, because that is often

---

3 Paulo Freire, *Pedagogy of the Oppressed* (London: Bloomsbury Publishing, 2000), p. 71.

how teachers are trained to manage their classrooms. It is also the case that many teachers teach in the same way they themselves were taught.

In a blogging context, it is easy to be offended when an adverse comment is received on your blog. You may be tempted to respond aggressively, to 'put the other person right'. Often though, good learning occurs when we consider the views of others. Even if we don't agree with the views of other people, it is good to consider them, to evaluate their meaning and contemplate alternative perspectives.

Dialogue is one of the most powerful affordances of blogging.

2. Don't be afraid to speak out on your blog about issues that concern you. Freire counsels: 'Washing one's hands of the conflict between the powerful and the powerless means to side with the powerful, not to be neutral.' Clearly there is plenty of inequality in the world, some of which exists within the world of education. Schools are not perfect, and there is no education system in the world that has it completely correct.

    There is no better place for speaking out against injustice or exposing inequalities than a popular blog site. It's the 21st century soap box. It's the digital version of Speakers' Corner. We could argue that it's as good as being the publisher of your own newspaper. People will read what you have to say if it's interesting, and it's even more powerful if your writing is passionate. So use your blog to speak out on behalf of those who can't speak out for themselves.

3. Use blogs to circumvent regulated learning. Students who blog quickly discover that they can explore knowledge for themselves. They realise they have it within them to become independent learners. Freire was critical of the banking approach to education, where teachers regulate learning: 'The teacher's task is to organise a process which already occurs spontaneously, to "fill" the students by making deposits of information which he or she considers constitutes true knowledge.'[4] When a learner starts to blog, they start to think

---

4   Paulo Freire, *Pedagogy of the Oppressed* (London: Bloomsbury Publishing, 2000), p. 57.

for themselves. They have to consider an audience of more than one (the teacher) and they are required to be masters of their own journey.

Blogging can subvert traditional education in another way. The dialogue that can ensue from blogging is often more valuable than the writing on the blog itself. Dave Mitchell's QuadBlogging[5] and Julia Skinner's 100 Word Challenge[6] are just two of the British school-based blogging projects that are now making a real difference for learners globally by providing them with a guaranteed audience every time they post a new blog. In QuadBlogging the students in one school undertake in the first week to write blogs, whilst three other schools read and comment. In the second week another school takes the responsibility to write, so that by the end of a month, students in all of the schools have had the opportunity to write, read and comment. The 100 Word Challenge works in a similar manner, providing an audience for children's work.

4.   Read other people's blogs and make comments. The act of seeking out alternative perspectives and counter views will in itself sharpen the reader's thinking and cause them to question received knowledge. Freire says: 'It is indispensable to analyse the contents of newspaper editorials following any given event. "Why do different newspapers have such different interpretations of the same fact?" This practice helps develop a sense of criticism, so that people will react to newspapers or new broadcasts not as passive objects of the "communiqués" directed at them, but rather as consciousnesses seeking to be free.'[7]

Alongside newspapers and news broadcasts we can add blog commentaries. They are considered to be 'grey' literature (that is, not formally peer reviewed) rather than 'white' literature, but they are useful indicators of popular views and public trends. Blogs are places where people can express their opinions and offer their interpretations, and in the digital age

---

5   See: www.quadblogging.com.
6   See: www.100wc.net.
7   Paulo Freire, *Pedagogy of the Oppressed* (London: Bloomsbury Publishing, 2000), p. 103.

these take the place of the street corners where individuals hold their conversations. Engaging with knowledge in this way can liberate the mind and help develop critical thought.

5.   Use blogging to support thinking. Often, abstract thoughts remain abstract unless they are externalised in some concrete form. Traditionally, writing has been used as a means to crystallise thinking, because as Daniel Chandler says: 'In the act of writing, we are written.' Freire writes: 'In all the stages of decoding, people exteriorise their view of the world.'[8] This implies that in order to understand our personal reality, we need to first bring our thoughts out into the open.

Blogs are public-facing tools that enable their owners to externalise their thinking in a way that is both stylistic and open for scrutiny. In the act of public writing, we expose our ideas and begin to understand our own thoughts more clearly.

6.   Use blogging as reflection. Reflection is an important part of learning, and is a skill that must be developed if it is to lead to successful outcomes. Reflection is also the key to personal liberation. Freire argues: 'Attempting to liberate the oppressed without their reflective participation in the act of liberation is to treat them as objects which must be saved from a burning building.'[9]

Reflection means active participation in learning, and blogging is a very powerful tool to support this process.

Freinet and social media

Another great theorist who did much to reform education systems around the globe is the lesser known French educator Célestin Freinet. He died in 1966, when we were only just beginning to realise that computers might be more than mere calculating machines. If he could see them now, what might Freinet make of

---

8   Paulo Freire, *Pedagogy of the Oppressed* (London: Bloomsbury Publishing, 2000), p. 87

9   Paulo Freire, *Pedagogy of the Oppressed* (London: Bloomsbury Publishing, 2000), p. 47.

today's digital technologies? What would he have said about the use of social media or the mobile phone in education? He certainly believed in using technology to enhance learning, because he purchased and ran his own printing press.

Search the Web and you will find little about Freinet in English – most documents are in French. You will discover, however, that he cared deeply about holistic approaches to education and believed that the school system of his time was broken. Here are five of his then radical methods placed into the context of social media:

1. *The Pedagogy of Work.* Learners should be encouraged to learn through making products and providing services. This can be easily set up and conducted using Web 2.0 tools. What better way to encourage students to engage in learning a topic than to get them to make something that represents the topic they are learning? An extension to this would be to facilitate their engagement in the commercial world. What would happen if students were encouraged to create services and products and then sell them?

   Several schools are already doing this. One or two keep small farms that yield produce which can be sold at market. Others support their students to develop apps or other digital stuff which can be sold online through established retailers. Students could find out about how e-commerce works by selling on eBay or Amazon. Social media makes this process a great deal easier, but teachers of younger students should ensure that their safety is protected.

2. *Enquiry-based Learning Method.* Learning by asking questions is not only fun, it's effective. But we can't always get every answer right at the first attempt. Learners need to learn in a psychologically safe environment where they have permission to fail, and to learn from that failure. One of the most familiar environments for students is in game-based learning. Video games, especially those that are social, and where they get to work, solving problems and challenges, and play within a team or guild, teach them a great number of transferable skills such as problem solving, team work, dexterity, creative thinking, negotiation of meaning, patience and persistence.

Enquiry-based learning, too, can be incorporated into this kind of scenario, with many games posing problems and challenges for users to overcome. Students need to understand and answer the questions before they can gain more points, or proceed to the next level of the game.

This is education by stealth.

3. *Co-operative Learning Method.* Learners can cooperate not only in the production processes and game-playing outlined above, they can also cooperate or even collaborate on the team-based creation of blogs, wikis, or video production. All of these can be created by the team and then posted online for an audience to appreciate, evaluate and discuss. As has been shown repeatedly in long-running projects such as QuadBlogging, giving students an audience for their work encourages them to hone their writing skills, develop and improve their presentation skills and gain an appreciation of performing their learning for an audience. The benefits of blogging are wide ranging, and when it is developed into cooperative projects it can have a great motivational power.

4. *The Natural Method.* Students learn best when they are naturally interested in the topic, and the level of success increases when learning takes place in authentic and realistic contexts. Facebook and other social networking tools are great for connecting people, and most students can use their accounts effectively to do this. Some may think of extending their connections to students in other parts of the world. This would be an extension of the pen pal method used many years ago, where schools paired students with those in other schools. They then wrote to each other regularly, and learnt all about each other's cultures, backgrounds and traditions.

   · Using social networking tools to promote e-pal conversations could potentially spread worldwide, with students in different countries discovering about foreign lands, cultures, languages, geography, history, music and sport.

5. *The Democratic Method.* Students learn about fairness, celebrating diversity, choice, friendship, relationships and a whole host of other human experiences and challenges through an appreciation of their entire community. They can

take responsibility for their own choices and actions and understand how they fit into their community (locally and globally) through connecting with others using social media tools.

This process can be aided through the use of voting tools, aggregation tools such as Digg, Diigo and Delicious, and curation tools such as Pearltrees and Scoop.it; the same applies to the 'like' and '+1' buttons of Facebook and Google Plus. Getting them to make decisions democratically enables them to understand that their opinion counts, but it must always be considered in the wider context of the community.

Illich and the Social Web

Ivan Illich was a renowned anarchist philosopher and intellectual maverick. A former Roman Catholic priest, he was arguably one of the most outspoken and prescient of 20th century critical theorists, and his work continues to gain traction now that technology is pervading every aspect of our lives. Illich hoped for a time when the transmission model of education, which he described as 'funnels', would be replaced by 'educational webs' – his pre-digital concept that is now recognisable as social networks. At the start of the 1970s Illich wrote:

> The current search for new educational funnels must be reversed into the search for their institutional inverse: educational webs which heighten the opportunity for each one to transform each moment of his living into one of learning, sharing, and caring.[10]

In the context of the technology of his day, Illich saw networked computers and telephone systems being used to encourage and promote exchanges of ideas, knowledge and expertise. Illich was not a big fan of traditional education, at least not in the form he observed. He advocated a participatory form of education that democratised knowledge and privileged learning over teaching, and saw technology as a means to transform education.

---

10 Ivan Illich, *Deschooling Society* (London: Penguin, 1971).

What would Illich have made of the Social Web? We will never know, because he died in 2002, just as Web 2.0 was emerging. Yet his work gives the impression that he would have welcomed it heartily and would have been one of its strongest advocates for education. Ivan Illich envisioned a community (or network) of learners that was self-sufficient. Here is his vision for how it might be achieved:

> The operation of a peer-matching network would be simple. The user would identify himself by name and address and describe the activity for which he sought a peer. A computer would send him back the names and addresses of all those who had inserted the same description. It is amazing that such a simple utility has never been used on a broad scale for publicly valued activity.[11]

Today we see this vision realised by millions. In so many ways, the social Web mirrors Illich's ideas for 'information exchanges' and 'peer matching' services, especially where facilitated through mobile, Internet-enabled personal devices. Never before has knowledge been generated and shared globally on such a scale as we see today on the Web. Video, audio, text and status updates are being uploaded to the Web every second of every day, by innumerable users.

Illich saw people as naturally itinerant in their learning, roaming where they wished, encountering knowledge serendipitously and interacting with each other in an informal manner to learn reciprocally. This was a long way away from the oppressive state-controlled education systems he railed so strongly against. Deschooling society, in Illich's own terms, was not about doing away with education, but of discarding the moribund rituals and restrictive practices that epitomised formal schooling. These ideals were captured in quite pragmatic architectural and city planning terms by Alexander et al.[12] when they conceived of a society where community leaders could:

> ... work in piecemeal ways to decentralize the process of learning and enrich it through contact with many places and people all over the city.

They list a range of actors and events that could facilitate this, including the use of workshops, teachers who work from home or

---

11 Ibid.
12 C. Alexander, S. Ishikawa and M. Silverstein, *A Pattern Language: Towns, Buildings, Construction* (Oxford: Oxford University Press, 1977).

travel, other professionals willing to take on the young as helpers, older children teaching younger children, visits to museums, as well as scholarly seminars, industrial workshops, and enlisting the support of senior citizens too. They argue that the way forward would be to:

> Build new educational facilities in a way which extends and enriches this network.

Such a move in society would radically depart from the centralised services that are familiar in today's inner cities. However, informal learning does already exist in the form of collectives, adult education classes, informal exchanges, and even the emerging hacker and maker cultures. Illich saw informal learning, especially that which was situated and authentic, as being more meaningful than education that was being imposed upon learners from above, saying: 'Most learning is not the result of instruction. It is rather the result of unhampered participation in a meaningful setting.'[13]

In his later work entitled *Tools for Conviviality,* Illich[14] began to expose some of the societal trends and excavated the role technology would play in shaping work. He saw people as inherently creative, but like so many other neo-Marxist philosophers,[15] he was acutely aware of the dangers of automation and blind obedience to technology, arguing that the role of the artisan holds greater significance than that of the unthinking operator:

> People need new tools to work with rather than tools that 'work' for them.[16]

Social media, especially those that enable users to create and share content, fall into the category of tools that are worked by us. They tap into the essence of our individual creativity, providing us with blank canvases upon which we can express our ideas and share our thoughts. It is likely that Illich would have welcomed the notion of user-generated content, and would have applauded the role of social media in challenging and undermining the megalithic capitalist industries of our time. He would no doubt also have warned us about the danger of enslaving ourselves to social

---

13 Ivan Illich, *Deschooling Society* (London: Penguin, 1971).

14 Ivan Illich, *Tools for Conviviality* (New York: Harper and Row, 1973).

15 Harry Braverman, *Labor and Monopoly Capital* (New York: Monthly Review Press, 1974).

16 Ivan Illich, *Tools for Conviviality* (New York: Harper and Row, 1973), p. 10.

networking tools, and would have expressed cynicism over the blatant advertising cultures that surround them. In the final analysis, however, many of Illich's visions are materialising in the digital age, and I believe he would have been gratified to see them come to fruition.

The preceding is mostly speculative, but an appreciation of the finer nuances of Illich's writings indicate to us that he would certainly not have rejected the role social media can play in advancing and enriching education. It remains to be seen to what extent social media and other technologies might play a role in the transformation of the centralised, state-funded education system.

Recycling Kolb

Most learning professionals have heard of David A. Kolb. His experiential learning model[17] is just one part of his grander theory of learning, and is often cited as a model that encapsulates the entire learning journey. Kolb's model was categorised by Mayes and de Freitas[18] as an individual constructivist theory, in that it features a number of components that reflect solo learning activities. It owes much to Piaget's 'scientific' or cognitive constructivist camp, and is in direct contrast to the more familiar social constructivist theories of Vygotsky and Bruner, which rely on co-construction and negotiation of meaning.

Kolb's model encompasses individual exploration of the world, and can be seen in a number of activities such as problem-based learning, enquiry-based learning and experiential learning. Although none of these preclude a social element of learning, such as collaboration or group discussion, the individual, cognitive constructivism espoused by Piaget tends to rely on the ability of the learner to be an autonomous and independent self-learner.

The experiential model Kolb proposed reveals a particular flow of activity that is represented in the image below. It flows clockwise and

---

17 David A. Kolb, *Experiential Learning: Experience as the Source of Learning and Development* (Englewood Cliffs NJ: Prentice-Hall, 1984).
18 Terry Mayes and Sara de Freitas, 'Review of e-Learning Theories, Frameworks and Models', *JISC e-Learning Models Desk Study* 1 (2004).

is both iterative and cyclical. It is representative of the kind of activities one sees in the old style e-learning package designs still used in many companies to impart basic health and safety or customer care training.

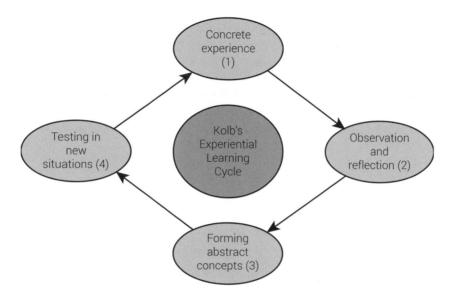

Kolb's experiential learning cycle

One of the criticisms of Kolb's model is that it is fairly prescriptive, and from it derives the four learning styles he identified; diverging, assimilating, converging and accommodating.

A number of derivative models such as Honey and Mumford's Learning Styles Inventory[19] 'borrowed' from this model. It continues to feature strongly in many corporate training/learning and development (L and D) design and delivery strategies because it focuses largely on competence and performance – traits most businesses value and require their employees to acquire and develop. And yet, although L and D departments are also embracing social learning, many still continue to refer to Kolb's model as an important model of learning.

---

19 Peter Honey and Alan Mumford, *Using Your Learning Styles* (Maidenhead: Peter Honey, 1986).

Some might consider this questionable. One view is that the experiential learning model is increasingly irrelevant in an age where social media and social learning are growing in prominence. In light of this it is worth revisiting Kolb's model to explore its criticisms and weaknesses.

One major criticism of Kolb's experiential learning cycle is that any or all of the four phases he identifies could occur simultaneously.[20] Another is that the model does not sufficiently acknowledge the power of reflection on learning.[21] Probably the most important criticism of Kolb's cycle is that depending on the learner, and/or the activities they are engaged in, some stages of the process can be bypassed, or repeated several times in any sequence, especially using technology that supports reiteration.

Back in 1933 John Dewey[22] remarked that reflective learning processes are highly complex and as Smith[23] has further argued, trying to represent this complexity in such neat and precise units is overly simplistic and clearly problematic. There is little to stop the process Kolb describes being reversed or sequenced in an entirely different way, depending on learner motivation, individual differences, or the subject being studied. Furthermore, there is a new component Kolb probably had no reason to consider at the time: the digital tools being employed to support those learning activities.

I also believe that besides there being very little (or mostly weak) empirical evidence to support Kolb's model (and all of its derivatives), in a digital age it is now just about obsolete. Kolb's model served its purpose in the 'instructional design' period of e-learning development where 'stand alone' computer based training (CBT) content was king, but we have moved on. Social learning processes, especially those mediated through social media, are showing greater promise than isolated learning, and we now have the tools to capitalise on the human instinct to connect with others, learn

---

20 M. Jeffs and T. Smith, *Learning from Experience* (1999). Available online at: http://www.infed.org/foundations/f-explrn.htm.
21 David Boud, Rosemary Keogh and David Walker, *Reflection: Turning Experience into Learning* (Abingdon: Routledge, 1985): 52–68.
22 John Dewey, *How We Think* (Boston: Heath, 1933).
23 M. K. Smith, *David A. Kolb on Experiential Learning* (2001). Available online at: http://www.infed.org/biblio/b-explrn.htm.

collaboratively, and to create, remix and share our own content. Kolb's model seems anachronistic, belonging to another time.

As we have already seen, theorists are now developing new models to explain the processes that occur when people learn using socially rich interactive digital media.

5
Rebooting Learning

Don't limit a child to your own learning, for he was born in another time.

Rabindranath Tagore

We know that learning is changing. By this, I don't mean that learning is changing at a fundamental, neurological level. Rather, I'm pointing out that there is evidence of a shift in the way students discover, create and share knowledge. As Wikipedia founder Jimmy Wales has suggested, we are now living in a new era of participation, where everyone can contribute to the world's knowledge. As we have seen, technology creates a number of new possibilities, especially for personalised and self-regulated learning. Although there is nothing new about people unearthing their own knowledge and directing their own learning, the scale of personalised learning is unprecedented. This ethos emerges in movements such as Edupunk – a do-it-yourself approach to education – and in the creation of personal learning environments, the hacker movement and the rise in popularity of open source software. Such new tools and opportunities will inevitably exert an influence on traditional education.

As we saw in previous chapters, reconceptualisation of knowledge is an important characteristic of learning in the digital age. This suggests a reappraisal of many of the older theories of how knowledge was structured, and how education has previously been conducted. The older theories still have much to offer teachers, but new questions are being asked about how knowledge is represented, and how learning can be supported in formal settings. Some pedagogical theories have been useful in the past to explain how learning progresses and becomes more complex as the learner builds on their knowledge and experience.

On the face of it, these theories offer explanations that are convenient and easy to accept. But doing so does not make them sound. In this chapter, I will explore some of the theories and models that have gained wide acceptance in education over the years, and expose some of their inherent problems.

Bloom and bust

Bloom's Taxonomy has been hailed as a template for best practice in course design. It has been a part of the bedrock of teacher education courses for over half a century, and is a model just about every learning professional is aware of and has used at some point in their teaching career.

Benjamin Bloom and his colleagues originally identified three distinct domains of learning: the Cognitive (thinking – knowing, reasoning), Affective (feeling – emotions, attitudes) and Psychomotor (doing – physical skills, practice). The Cognitive domain[1] and Affective domain[2] taxonomies were published as edited volumes, in 1956 and 1964 respectively. Bloom's Cognitive Taxonomy is probably the best known and most used of the taxonomies, and is organised into Bloom's Cognitive Taxonomy six levels with learning rising from simple to complex. These are often represented pictorially as a pyramid with the most complex category of cognitive gain at the apex.

---

1 B. S. Bloom and D. R. Krathwohl, *Taxonomy of Educational Objectives: The Classification of Educational Goals, Handbook I: Cognitive Domain* (New York: Longmans, 1956).

2 B. S. Bloom, D. R. Krathwohl and B. B. Masia, *Taxonomy of Educational Objectives: The Classification of Educational Goals, Handbook II: Affective Domain* (New York: David McKay Company, 1964).

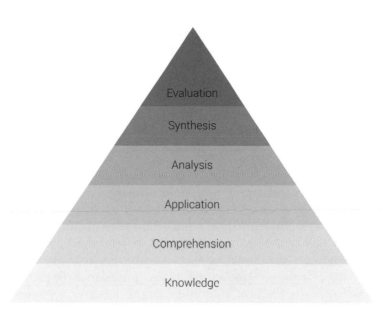

Bloom's Cognitive Taxonomy

In the past, the usefulness of the model has been widely acknowledged. Many have used the taxonomy as a template to apply escalating difficulty to learning objectives in course design.

More recently, Bloom's Taxonomy has come under close scrutiny, revealing some serious questions. How relevant is it in the digital age? Should we continue to organise learning experiences as a gradient of 'terminal learning objectives' in an era where learning is changing, and where personal technologies and social media are increasingly significant?

Assessment methods are changing too. For many teachers Bloom's Cognitive Taxonomy represented a prescriptive method of control over 'learning behaviour', and offered structure for education in the last century. But just how desirable is it in today's classrooms? Exactly how much control do teachers need to exert over students' learning today? Shouldn't there be more freedom to learn, and to express individual creativity? Where do these components fit into the grand scheme of 21st century learning?

If you subscribe to the belief that students are *tabulae rasae* – blank slates on which knowledge can be inscribed by experts – then you are likely to see plenty of merit in Bloom's Taxonomy. If, on the other hand, you believe that all learners have the ability to be creative, critical and independent, then you may start looking elsewhere for guidance on how to provide engaging learning experiences.

Criticism of Bloom's Cognitive Taxonomy has been widespread. Bloom and his colleagues identified three domains – knowledge, attitudes and skills – but omitted some important parallel components, such as intuition and creativity. Was this because they are difficult to 'measure' objectively?

There are other problems too. It is usually a mistake to try to represent complex ideas in the form of simplistic diagrams but most of us still find it convenient. It is uncertain whether Bloom and his colleagues ever wished to see their work represented as a pyramid (it was originally presented as an escalating linear sequence), but that is how it now appears in many popular interpretations. Portraying the six levels of attainment in this manner only serves to reinforce the prescriptive, sequential and reductionist nature of Bloom's Cognitive Taxonomy.

Shelly Wright[3] expresses disquiet about this, suggesting that in the pyramid model it seems that to reach a peak of creativity learners first need to traverse all the inferior stages of learning. This is clearly untrue in many real life experiences. Wright suggests flipping or inverting the pyramid so that creating (or making) becomes the first stage in the learning process. I'm not convinced that inverting the pyramid would significantly improve the taxonomy. It simply creates yet another linear, artificial representation of complex learning processes.

Furthermore, there is doubt over both the validity and reliability of Bloom's Taxonomy, as discussed in Sugrue's critique.[4] Ormell[5] criticised Bloom for failing to acknowledge 'imaginative understanding' – another way of saying creativity in learning.

And so Bloom's Taxonomy has come under fire for its simplistic view of a very complex human activity. Postmodernist criticism points to

3 Shelly Wright, 'Flipping Bloom's Taxonomy' (2012). Available online at: http://plpnetwork.com/2012/05/15/flipping-blooms-taxonomy/.

4 Brenda Sugrue, 'Problems with Bloom's Taxonomy' (2002). Available online at: http://eppicinc.files.wordpress.com/2011/08/sugrue_bloom_critique_perfxprs.pdf.

5 C. P. Ormell, 'Bloom's Taxonomy and the Objectives of Education', *Educational Research* 17 (1974).

its sterile and ordered classification of learning modes and argues that the human mind is far too complex to be represented in such a prescribed, organised manner. Another contemporary critique is that many of the terms used in the taxonomy are artificially constructed as ideology to 'conceal the messy side of learning'.[6]

Probably the most telling criticism of Bloom's Taxonomy though – and the most relevant in the social media age – is that the taxonomy tends to focus on individual learning activities. Although individual learning remains important, social learning, especially when supported by technology, is increasingly prevalent in all sectors of education. Collaboration, shared online spaces, discussion, co-construction of content and negotiation of meaning are all evident in many learning contexts, both formal and informal. A plausible conclusion might be that Bloom's Taxonomy seems to have less relevance in today's technology-rich flexible learning environments. It was devised in an era of instruction in which drill and practice were commonly accepted in education and where behaviourism was the dominant ideology.

Ultimately, Bloom's Taxonomy has been used as a tool to aid curriculum design. However, it is nonsense to expect teachers to continue to write verb-laden 'instructional objectives' to describe behaviour for each and every one of the six cognitive levels that they are subsequently required to measure. At best, applying the taxonomy to assessment reduces learning to a series of fairly meaningless behavioural links, and at worst, it does nothing to support or encourage children's intuitive and creative instincts.

---

6 John T. Spencer, 'Bloom's Taxonomy: Criticisms. Teacher Commons' (2008). Available online at: http://teachercommons.blogspot.co.uk/2008/04/bloom-taxonomy-criticisms.html.

Bloom reheated

In the age of digital media, where learners create, remix and share their own content, some consider that an overhaul of Bloom's Cognitive Taxonomy was long overdue. Unfortunately, Lorin Anderson's revised version of the taxonomy, which he devised in conjunction with Krathwohl,[7] does little to improve the original model. Supposedly upgraded to take into consideration new ways of learning using digital tools, the revised model remains firmly rooted in the old behaviourist paradigm, and seems to be just as reliant on the production of observable, and therefore measurable, behaviour as the original model.

This is unsurprising given that Anderson is one of Bloom's former students, and Bloom was steeped in the behaviourist tradition. However, one useful feature of Anderson's model is that it diverts the focus away from declarative knowledge (knowing that) toward procedural knowledge (knowing how), and this is useful in Constructionist learning contexts. Constructionism is learning by making, an approach based on the work of Seymour Papert.[8] If students learn facts but have no understanding of how or why these facts can be applied, or how they can be constructed into some useful form, learning is two-dimensional at best.

---

7 Lorin Anderson and D. R. Krathwohl (eds.), *A Taxonomy for Learning, Teaching and Assessing: A Revision of Bloom's Taxonomy of Educational Objectives* (London: Longman, 2001).

8 Seymour Papert, *Mindstorms: Children, Computers and Powerful Ideas* (Brighton: Harvester Press, 1980).

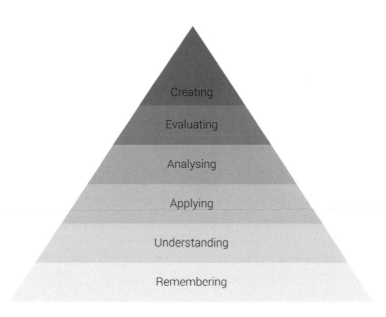

Bloom's Revised Cognitive Taxonomy

One of the gravest errors in Anderson's revised model is that it's still a taxonomy, and a flawed taxonomy at that. Anderson's new categorisation simply shuffles the original categories around a little. He places 'Creating' at the apex of the pyramid, with 'Evaluating' beneath it. Overbaugh and Schultz[9] suggest that in Anderson's model, Bloom's 'Synthesis' is replaced by 'Creating', and that Bloom's 'Evaluation' and 'Synthesis' therefore trade places. This prompts a question: should we really expect learners to create something and then not bother to evaluate it? Why the swap?

The problem actually lies in the structure and sequence.

Ultimately, it is not possible to represent synthesis and evaluation, or any of the other levels of cognitive achievement as a single linear process. Let's suppose instead that learning processes are chaotic and iterative in nature, and that we learn through a continual flux of categories combined in increasingly complex ways. We might acquire better knowledge while we are in the process of applying and evaluating. This leads to the conclusion that the classification of levels of attainment is misrepresented in both Bloom's and Anderson's models.

---

9 R. C. Overbaugh and L. Schultz 'Bloom's Taxonomy' (2005). Available online at: http://ww2.odu.edu/educ/roverbau/Bloom/blooms_taxonomy.htm.

Tim Brook makes the point that the sequence of learning categories is problematic and suggests a matrix instead. But this still fails to address the problem that Bloom's Taxonomy segregates and compartmentalises activities, when often we learn across and through combinations and reiterations of learning modes.

Neither Bloom's nor Anderson's model takes account of new, fluid methods of learning. Emerging theories such as Connectivism, Heutagogy and Paragogy are more representative of digital age learning, and for many the future of learning through digital tools will rely heavily upon such explanatory frameworks.

Teachers need to find ways to nurture the agile, flexible, critical and creative learners that are desperately needed in our communities today. Neither Bloom's nor Anderson's taxonomy has the explanatory power or flexibility to achieve this. Patching up an old model and rehashing it is not sufficient. As Paul McCartney once remarked: 'You can't reheat a soufflé.'

The digital natives discourse

One of the more controversial theories of the digital age is the claim that technology is rewiring our brains.[10] Some also claim that prolonged use of the Web is detrimental to human intellectual development.[11] It could be argued that these theories stem back to the seminal claim of Marshall McLuhan that 'we shape our tools, and thereafter our tools shape us'.

This belief was also the basis for the Digital Natives and Immigrants theory,[12] a persistent discourse that has greatly influenced the thinking of educators in recent years. A significant body of work has surrounded this theory, including descriptions of younger students

---

10 Susan Greenfield, *The Quest For Identity In The 21st Century* (London: Sceptre, 2009).
11 Nicholas Carr, *The Shallows: What the Internet is Doing to Our Brains* (New York: W. W. Norton & Company, 2011).
12 Marc Prensky, 'Digital Natives, Digital Immigrants', *On the Horizon* 9.5 (2001).

as 'the Net Generation',[13] 'Screenagers',[14] 'Born Digital',[15] 'Millennials',[16] and even 'Homo Zappiens'. The latter label suggests that younger students learn differently, through searching rather than through absorbing, through externalising rather than through internalising information. It argues that they are better at multitasking, and see no separation between playing and learning.[17]

If these theories accurately represent 21st century learning, and younger students do learn differently, the implications for education are profound, demanding changes in the way formal learning content is developed, delivered and organised, and a reappraisal of our conception of knowledge and what it means for education.

Inevitably, of course, there are objections to the Digital Natives theory.

All of these theorists tend to characterise younger learners as being different to previous generations in their use of technology. This position is countered by researchers who maintain that such claims are largely based on anecdotal and seemingly intuitive arguments. Commentators who oppose the Digital Natives theory argue that there is no significant difference in the way younger or older students manage their online learning activities[18] and that the current generation of learners is far from homogenous and there is no clear evidence that multitasking is a new phenomenon and exclusively the preserve of younger learners.[19] Jones and Healing[20] criticise the Digital Natives and Immigrants theory for being too

---

13 Don Tapscott, *Growing up Digital: The Rise of the Net Generation* (New York: McGraw Hill, 1998).

14 Douglas Rushkoff, *Playing the Future: What We Can Learn from Digital Kids* (London: HarperCollins, 1996).

15 J. Palfrey and U. Gasser, *Born Digital: Understanding the First Generation of Digital Natives* (New York: Basic Books, 2008).

16 Diane Oblinger, 'Boomers, Gen-xers, and Millennials: Understanding the New Students', *Educause Review*. 38.4 (2003).

17 Wim Veen and Ben Vrakking, *Homo Zappiens: Growing up in a Digital Age* (London: Network Continuum Education, 2006).

18 Charles Crook and C. Harrison, *Web 2.0 Technologies for Learning at Key Stages 3 and 4* (Coventry: Becta Publications, 2008).

19 S. Bennett, K. Maton and L. Kervin, 'The 'Digital Natives' Debate: A Critical Review of the Evidence', *British Journal of Educational Technology*, 39, 5 (2008): 775–786.

20 Chris Jones and G. Healing, 'Net Generation Students: Agency and Choice and the New Technologies', *Journal of Computer Assisted Learning*, 26.3 (2010): 344–356.

simplistic, and point out that a complexity exists which the theory ignores. Evidently, there are great variations in the way students of all ages use technology, and these cannot be based solely on generational differences, but are more likely to be the result of personal agency and choice.

There is yet further dissent. Vaidhyanathan[21] argues that 'there is no such thing as a digital generation.' He suggests that every generation has an equal distribution of individuals with low, medium and high levels of technology competency. Vaidhyanathan is uncomfortable with the erroneous misclassification of generations and associated assumptions of technology competency levels, and warns: 'We should drop our simplistic attachments to generations so we can generate an accurate and subtle account of the needs of young people – and all people, for that matter.'

Perhaps the most cogent remarks come from Neil Selwyn,[22] who argues that contrary to the populist beliefs expressed in the Digital Natives discourse, young people's engagement with technology is often far less spectacular.[23] According to Selwyn, accounts of Digital Natives are often based on anecdotal evidence, are inconsistent or exaggerated, and hold very little in common with the reality of technology use in the real world. A problem for the Digital Natives theory is that it tends to characterise older generations as being alienated from technology, while conversely, teachers can make dangerous assumptions about the sophisticated capabilities of young people.[24]

Selwyn counsels: 'Whilst inter-generational tensions and conflicts have long characterised popular understandings of societal progression, adults should not feel threatened by younger generations' engagements with digital technologies, any more than young people should feel constrained by the "pre-digital" structures of older generations.'[25]

---

21 S. Vaidhyanathan, 'Generational Myth: Not all Young People are Tech-Savvy', *The Chronicle of Higher Education* 55(4) (2008).

22 Neil Selwyn, 'The Digital Native: Myth and Reality', *Aslib Proceedings* 61.4 (2011): 364-379.

23 S. Livingstone, *Children and the Internet* (Oxford: Polity Press, 2009).

24 G. Kennedy, T. Judd, B. Dalgarnot and J. Waycott, 'Beyond Digital Natives and Immigrants: Exploring Types of Net Generation Students', *Journal of Computer Assisted Learning*, 26.5 (2010): 332–343.

25 Neil Selwyn, 'The Digital Native: Myth and Reality', *Aslib Proceedings* 61.4 (2011), p. 376.

Arguably the most useful explanatory framework for current online activities is offered by David White and Alison Le Cornu,[26] who have argued that habitual use of technology develops sophisticated digital skills regardless of the age of the user. They call these regular users 'digital residents' and describe them as being familiar and confident in the use of their chosen tools. On the other hand, those who are 'digital visitors' are less likely to be digitally adept or confident because of their casual or infrequent use of specific digital tools and services.

Teachers who fall into the visitors category for whatever reason tend to shy away from using technology in the classroom. If they subscribe to the digital natives and immigrants theory, they tend to have an expectation that their students will be more adept at using technology, and they will often consider themselves as novices. They may be tempted to fall back on old tried and tested methods, and for some this means standing at the front of the classroom and instructing. For students who are seeking a challenge, this is less than satisfactory. This is the point where students turn to their mobile phones and text each other under the tables. It's the modern day equivalent to passing notes in class. What does it take to engage the focus and attention of young people in today's education systems?

Challenge-based learning

You know that moment when you are in the zone, on the ball, your mind completely focused. You have become so engrossed in what you are doing that you forget what the time is, you forget to eat, you miss your sleep. You are in the flow, and nothing will distract you from the challenge that is before you. Often this is a state we find ourselves in when we are playing an absorbing game or reading a fascinating book. We are completely immersed in the experience, and nothing else matters.

That's essentially what flow is. According to Mihály Csíkszentmihályi, being in the flow is the ultimate in focused intrinsic motivation and

---

26 David White and Alison Le Cornu, 'Visitors and Residents: A New Typology for Online Engagement', *First Monday* 16.9 (2011). Available online at: http://firstmonday.org/ojs/index.php/fm/article/view/3171.

is the basis of optimal experience. In simplistic terms, being in flow is where students find themselves in that narrow channel between disinterest and fear. There is a fine balance between the challenge of the task and the skills the learner has at their disposal. Maintaining this balance avoids disillusionment if your skills don't measure up to the challenge or boredom if the task is too simple and easy to achieve. Csíkszentmihályi[27] describes three conditions under which this kind of flow can be achieved. In the context of education, learners need to be given clear goals, immediate feedback on their progress and performance, and a good balance between opportunity (the challenge) and their own capacity (or skills).

Students who are immersed in their games tend to be single-mindedly motivated to achieve their goals or reach the next level. They are in the flow. They assess their own performance against previous personal performances, and it is a most honest form of measurement. Generally, it's not hard to get young people to play games. Getting them to the place where they fall so in love with learning that little else matters is another issue entirely. One of the ways teachers can help students to focus more on their studies is by making learning so irresistible that there seems to be no other option than to pursue it.

Games and gamification seem to offer students the chance to discover a fine equilibrium between boredom and anxiety, as do other forms of immersive learning, such as role play, simulation and problem solving. It's a key principle of learning design. As long as the learning resource is designed to have the appropriate levels of challenge built into it, and these levels rise incrementally, students should maintain their interest.

The graphic below illustrates how this occurs. P2 and P3 are positions that should be traversed quickly if students are to remain in the flow. If the design of the game or challenge is good, it will ensure that students can maintain that fine homeostasis between anxiety and boredom.

---

27 Mihályi Csíkszentmihályi, *Flow: The Psychology of Optimal Experience* (New York: Harper & Row, 1990).

Adapted from: Csíkszentmihályi (1991) and Killi (2009)

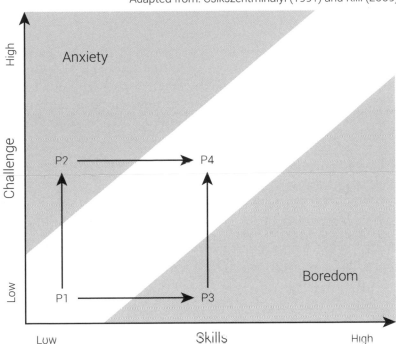

Csíkszentmihályi's flow theory

Adhering to Csíkszentmihályi's rubric, we see that successful challenge-based learning requires clearly defined and achievable goals that require some incremental development of skills beyond the average, and where the challenge rises commensurately to match those skills. Students also need timely feedback and if necessary, intervention. The student progresses from P1 to P4. If the subject matter is made interesting and enjoyable enough, teachers won't have to work too hard to encourage students to actively engage. Learners will do so naturally without any coercion. They will want to rise to the challenge and succeed because they want no other possible outcome.

Place this within a social context where students are pitting their skills and knowledge against others, or focusing their efforts for the good of a team they are proud to be a member of, either inside the classroom or beyond, and you can see how this might become a very powerful method of engaging them in learning.

Social games

Revisiting social constructivist theory, we find that the learner is situated in a wider network of learners that form a global community. This is often within a chat or gaming context. Their communication is technology mediated and users select their favourite digital tools to scaffold each other's learning within their communities of interest.

Often younger learners show less interest in using social networking sites such as Facebook or Twitter. These are where their parents and their teachers tend to congregate. Today's youth are more likely to be found gathering in games forums, wikis and sociable games such as League of Legends or World of Warcraft, spaces in which connection and collaboration are vital for success. In the gaming culture, this can involve not only the playing of the game, but also hacking into games, finding and sharing shortcuts and cheats, modding (using code to modify games or create new versions), voting and discussion. They also gain a sense of self-esteem and belonging by building their reputations through joining guilds and teams. Learning is constant, and is also constantly assessed.

These are clear reasons why games should neither be ignored nor dismissed as irrelevant in formal education. Great success has been achieved in the teaching of all curriculum subjects through the use of games, such as Guitar Hero (organisational skills, teamwork and communication skills), Angry Birds (mathematics, physics, trajectories) and even Grand Theft Auto, which has been used to teach children about citizenship and the problems caused by crime.[28] Ultimately, playing the game is the vehicle that transports the players to learning.

Playing social games online can exert a very powerful effect on the minds of users. They enter the sphere as novices and work their way incrementally towards expertise by solving problems, playing against others, using joint efforts and teamwork, and by constantly trying to better their own scores. This kind of assessment of their learning is ipsative, self-regulated and personalised. Emerging cultural and linguistic nuances are available to support learning that is useful in

---

28 Graeme Paton, 'Grand Theft Auto Used to Turn Children Against Crime', *The Telegraph*, 9 April, 2011.

sustaining the game-playing community. Players learn by trial and error, and build on their skills through learning from failure, practice and the observation of others.

The suspension of reality that features in many online social games becomes a sort of psychological safety net within which failure is an option, and where learning from that failure strengthens the skills and knowledge that are acquired. Transient zones of proximal development appear and then disappear as learning expands through and across the community. Social support appears and dissipates and more often than not, this support is now represented in the form of technology.

The games we play

Games-based learning is effective for a number of reasons. Firstly, there is an impressive array of transferable skills to be acquired, especially if the games played are designed effectively. Secondly, most people now have the capability to play games on the move, using smartphones, touchscreen tablets and handheld consoles. Thirdly, as we have already seen, many online games have very rich social dimensions, which lead gamers to extend their learning further through discussion, collaboration and competition.

Many scholars have researched the effects of games on learning, but probably one of the most prolific and profound games-based learning researchers is James Paul Gee. Gee has proposed several principles that together constitute a games-based learning theory.[29] The first is the psychological moratorium principle, which could also be referred to as the 'suspension of reality'. Gamers are free to take risks in spaces where 'real world' consequences are negated. In a first person shooter game, for example, you can kill as many enemies as you wish, and you won't be prosecuted for murder. You can fall from the top of a building or endure a high speed car crash, but you won't suffer a scratch or a bruise. You simply get back up and live to fight another day.

---

29 James Paul Gee, *What Video Games Have to Teach Us About Learning and Literacy* (New York: Palgrave Macmillan, 2003).

There is also the committed learning principle, which describes how gamers have sustained engagement as extensions of their real-world identities in relation to their virtual identities (or avatars). This often enables gamers to develop an emotional attachment for which they feel some sense of commitment, and this also makes the virtual world they inhabit more compelling. Lots of effort and practice invested in World of Warcraft or The Sims results from the gamer being committed – some might even say hooked – to the game.

Another equally important principle is the identity principle, which relates closely to the committed learning principle above. Learning through games often involves manipulation of identity in such a way that the gamer has real choice over how they wish to represent themselves, particularly in social games. This can result in forms of role playing where the gamer can choose to be a hero, a villain, or something entirely different.

The self-knowledge principle relates to virtual worlds (or games terrains) being constructed in such a way that gamers learn not only about that environment, but also about themselves and their current skills, knowledge and capabilities.

As has been previously stressed, gamers can make mistakes and learn from them. No one ever really fails, they just find a better way to reach the next level of the game. Each time, they improve their performance and avoid the same errors. As Graham Brown-Martin once remarked, gaming is powerful because there is constant assessment of performance. Usually this is self-assessment, but if it is a social game feedback also comes from the community who are playing the game.

Perhaps one of the most powerful principles is the achievement principle, which is instrumental in bringing many gamers back time and time again to improve their scores, hone their skills and relive previous experiences within the game. There are intrinsic rewards within most games, which if designed cleverly will provide a gradient of difficulty (levels and goals), including problems to solve and knowledge to gather, which gamers can achieve with incremental effort and commitment. This helps gamers to build on their problem solving and critical thinking skills, which are essential for successful learning and working.

There are several other principles identified by Gee, but I believe the ones listed above provide a reasonably clear explanation as to why games are so powerful, and why they should be seriously considered as tools to support learning for the 21st century. Increasingly, as communities of practice rely on technologies such as social media and games to propagate new forms of knowledge and promote better learning, another question emerges about the functionality of our tools. Can technology help us to think more clearly?

Cognitive technologies

We all need to think clearly, especially in times of duress, or where aspects of life are changing rapidly. As the world moves past and around us, we often find ourselves immersed in our digital worlds, ear buds in, our vision locked to a screen. We are surrounded by devices and tools, feeding us endless streams of content, all of which compete for our attention as we stand in the real world. It's often difficult to keep up when you are being constantly impacted by streams of new information, and one could easily feel overwhelmed by the relentless flow – this is a common experience for hundreds of millions of people across the globe. The cognitive energy we invest in all of this attention should produce something that is valuable. How can we quantify it, and how can it be harnessed toward productive outcomes?

The tools we now call on to help us learn and teach can be described as cognitive technologies – mind tools that help us to learn new things, to seek out new ideas and new concepts, and to boldly take us where we have not been before. They not only provide us with all the information, knowledge and learning we will ever need, they actually shape our minds in new ways too. Canadian media theorist Marshall McLuhan[30] wasn't the only one to notice the effect media have on thinking. Where McLuhan saw the movie as a medium that transports us from the linear toward configuration (of speed, space and time), he also believed that it is often the attributes of the medium, rather than its content, that shape our expectations. McLuhan never lived to see the Web, but if he had, he would no

---

30 Quentin Fiore and Marshall McLuhan, *The Medium is the Massage* (New York: Random House, 1967).

doubt have seen the extension of hyperlinked affordances toward non-linearity and beyond.

This poses a further question: have the multi-dimensional possibilities of the Web forged a generation of non-linear thinkers, or has the Web simply been fashioned in such a way that it reflects the natural structure of human minds? Such a conveniently synergetic relationship between mind and tool sometimes makes it difficult to see where the join might be between functionality and perception. Mind technology it certainly is, and it is also richly social. We would be poorer without it. With it, we can be enslaved or we can be liberated. Whichever direction we choose, there will be hundreds of millions of others to keep us company.

Canadian academic Alec Couros recently remarked: if you think the Web is simply a place to look up information, you are sadly mistaken.

Alec is right. The Web is a large learning space where we encounter others also interested in the same topics. It is a limitless place where people create and share knowledge, and it is a space in which we can have conversations that can continue almost indefinitely, drawing others into the dialogue from diverse interests, cultures and backgrounds. Content is merely one facet of the Web. Conversation is another, and it is probably a much more important component. The future of learning will be found not just in good curricula and content, but in communities of learning, a topic that will be dealt with in the next chapter.

6

A 21st Century Curriculum

Education is not a matter of life and death. It's much more important than that.

Bill Shankly (almost)

I flew into Cyprus a few years ago to give an invited speech at a conference. While I was there I discovered a dangerous game that is played in the tavernas. It's called Meze, and it's far more brutal than the Spanish tapas equivalent. There are two teams: the eating team and the waiter team. It starts in a very friendly manner when the eating team are shown to their tables – then the fun begins. The waiter team tries to beat the eating team into submission by delivering a constant supply of small dishes, containing far more food than they are ever likely to need in a full calendar month. It begins innocuously, with a few plates of pitta bread, houmous and tzatziki. The eating team is lulled into a false sense of security. This is nice, they think, we can do this.

Then more dishes begin to arrive at an alarming rate.

As the eating team finishes one dish, it is removed and *three* more replace it. The goal of the waiter team is to fill the table up so completely with food that there is no room left, and the eating team has no choice but to eat their way through the pile to safety.

The game is a fix. No matter how much the eating team consume, there are always more dishes arriving. Kebabs, eggplants, grilled cheese, prawns, skewered meat, fried octopus … You name it, it all arrives far too quickly. There is a sadistic streak in the waiter team. When they sense that the eating team has had enough, the waiter team continue to deliver knockout blows, even using the sneaky ploy of placing more food directly onto their plates.

Eventually, and inevitably, the eating team are writhing around in extreme agony on the floor clutching their stomachs and yelling 'Enough! We surrender!' The end of the game is signalled by the waving of a white napkin, and then you are able to observe the smug grins on the faces of the waiter team, who look at each other and nod knowingly. Oh yes, we have defeated yet another group of tourists with our clever and relentless food manoeuvres. Our job here is done.

Please may I leave the table?

Strangely, but not surprisingly, this led me to consider the world's education systems. Many are a little like the eating game of Meze. We pile the students' plates high with content. Content of every kind is presented to be consumed, and just like the Meze contestants, the poor students don't know what's coming next, and they don't stand a chance. Many are overwhelmed by the amount and diversity of content they need to learn, and the pace at which they are expected to learn it. Even while they are struggling their way through an overburdened 'just in case' curriculum, still more content continues to arrive at an alarming pace. Some learners cry out for mercy, but their voices go unheard and they are still compelled to consume the content, because later, they know they will be required to regurgitate it in a test to obtain their grades.

The summative examinations we see in schools bear little resemblance to that which will be required of students when they eventually go to work in the real world – no wonder so many wish to 'leave the table' early. What can teachers do to obviate this problem? Some are making a difference, reinterpreting the curriculum they are given by enabling activities and creating resources that facilitate student-centred learning. Learning at one's own pace, and in a manner that suits the individual will overcome some of the problems of overload, but more needs to be done.

Things are changing, but they are changing slowly; too slowly for many people's tastes. It's a dangerous game we are playing in education. It demands a rethink.

The 'just in case' curriculum

With the digital age upon us, I believe it is time educators and thought leaders reconsidered the way the school curriculum is structured and presented. The 'just in case' content laden curriculum model seems less meaningful and expedient in a world where just about any knowledge can be found on the Web.

My belief is that schools should be places where students can learn things that cannot be taught, or discovered alone. But as has already been discussed in some depth, schools are notoriously conservative and change is slow in coming. In state-funded schools content is still king, because 'content as curriculum' is easy and inexpensive to deliver, and that is what most governments require and impose. Yet, as many teachers know, this is not necessarily the best or the most effective approach.

When I went to school, my classmates and I were required to attend content-rich classes in mathematics, English language and literature, the sciences (physics, biology, chemistry), history, geography, music, art, religious education, craft and design, home economics, physical education, and languages (French and a choice of German or Latin) – all just in case we might need them later in life. Content was presented to me, and my job was to organise it in my head in such a way that when exams came around, I could represent it in a manner acceptable to the content experts.

I forgot much of that content once the exams were done. Notwithstanding, some knowledge did indeed become useful to me later in my life, and some would argue that nothing we learn is ever really wasted. And yet, how much more effective would our time in school have been if we had been given more problems to solve and challenges to meet, instead of content to consume?

Silo mentality

Another issue was that the subjects were unconnected to each other, and little attention was paid to what was learnt outside of the curriculum. The subjects were presented in distinct blocks of lessons, and no links between subjects were ever implied, let alone explicated. With the exception of a few subjects, my schooling didn't make that much sense to me.

Sadly, almost half a century later, little has changed for the schoolchildren of the 21st century.

Children are still required to learn a lot in school that is fact based. The connections between the subjects are ignored and subjects are still delivered separately. How many of the facts they are expected to memorise in lessons can be Googled? Do children really need to know what a phrasal verb is, or that William Shakespeare died in 1616, when what they really need to be able to do is write a coherent and convincing job application or construct a relevant CV?

Sir Ken Robinson, in his inimitable style during a TED Talk entitled 'How to Escape Education's Death Valley', made the following remark:

> If you sit kids down, hour after hour, doing low grade clerical work, don't be surprised when they start to fidget.[1]

Education should never be boring, and it should certainly always be challenging. Most importantly, learning should be relevant. The onus is on teachers to move school lessons away from low level, repetitive tasks towards high level, thought provoking challenges that continually engage children as they learn.

---

1 Sir Ken Robinson, 'How to Escape Education's Death Valley', TED Talks (April 2013). Available online at: http://www.ted.com/talks/ken_robinson_how_to_escape_education_s_death_valley.

Declarative knowledge

Content-based learning is known as declarative knowledge, because it is 'knowing that'. Put another way, it is the learning of facts and principles. This kind of knowledge has always found a place in education. And yet, in the so-called knowledge society where curriculum content has become increasingly mutable and open to challenge, our understanding of the world can change and facts can quickly become out of date. During my school years I was taught that there were nine planets in our solar system. Today we are told that Pluto is no longer a planet – now he is just a cartoon dog. Is it Myanmar or Burma? I was told by my geography teacher the Far Eastern country was called Burma. Then she was right, now she would be wrong. Is the atom still the smallest object known to humankind? No. A while back scientists discovered smaller things known as quarks, and something smaller still, called quantum foam. Apparently it's great for holding the universe together but pretty useless for a wet shave. What are we to make of all this? We can conclude that all knowledge is mutable, and subject to change.

Flipping the teacher

Over time, as our understanding changes and life becomes more ambiguous, some facts seem to become less concrete. Does this mean that teachers are wasting their own time and that of the children by teaching them facts which in a few years' time may be utterly out of date? Not necessarily, because teachers have to work with the curriculum of their day. However, all educators need to continue to challenge the idea that acquiring knowledge is the only goal of education.

Educators also need to maximise classroom contact time by supporting a spirit of discovery, where children develop their skills, competencies, and literacies too. This is the approach taken by adherents of flipping the classroom.

When Bergmann and Sams[2] first presented their concept of flipped classes they argued that assimilation of knowledge is much harder than instruction. Therefore, they reasoned, students should use technology to access content at home, learn it, and then return to the classroom where they can discuss it, reflect on it and deepen their understanding in the presence of subject experts. Many teachers are now flipping lessons, providing more interaction during contact time and transferring instruction and the transmission of content to technology outside of the classroom walls.

A radical version of the flipped concept is to switch the roles of teachers and learners. We have to learn deeply and gain a finer appreciation of our subject if we are teaching. If students are placed in situations where they need to present their learning, they are pushed to learn more deeply and critically. The teacher acts as their student, asking awkward questions and challenging what is presented, and students also gain more, not only in terms of what they have to learn but also in terms of feedback on their learning.

Skills for future work

Such pedagogy should be about supporting students as they consolidate their understanding and develop their critical thinking. Watching a video at home may help them to understand the principles of a theory or work out a maths problem. Writing a blog post and sharing it will help them to reflect on what they have learnt, and gain additional perspectives from their peers. Discussion later in the classroom with their peers and teacher will develop their understanding further, and help them to acquire the capability to work in teams, problem solve on the fly, and apply creative solutions. Such skills will be the common currency in the world of future work. Being able to think critically, connect with others and create a professional network will be the core competencies of the 21st century knowledge worker. 'Knowing how' – or procedural knowledge – will be just as great an asset as 'knowing that' for most young people.

---

2 Jon Bergmann and Aaron Sams, 'Flipping the Classroom', *Tech & Learning* 32.10 (2012): 42–43.

When he left school, my teenage son embarked on training to become a games designer. If, when I was his age, I had told my careers teacher that I wanted to be a games designer, he would probably have asked me whether I wanted to make cricket bats or footballs. Jobs are appearing that didn't exist even a year or two ago. Other jobs that people expected to be around for life are disappearing or already gone forever.

Why do some teachers still provide children with answers when all the answers are out there on the Web? Contemporary pedagogy is only effective if there is a clear understanding of the power and efficacy of the tools that are available. Shakespeare may well have died in 1616, but anyone can look this up on Wikipedia if and when they need to find out for themselves. A better skill would be to discern good from bad content on Wikipedia once you have searched and found it. This is one of the key digital literacies I will discuss in a later chapter.

Learning through questioning

All children are naturally curious. As they grow older, they ask questions about everything. My experience of school taught me that some teachers became irritated if we asked too many questions. It stopped them from getting on with the task of delivering content. Thankfully, that ethos is beginning to change. Enquiry-based learning is gradually taking hold in schools, but not quickly enough. Teachers should know that if they tap into the natural curiosity of children, they will inspire them to want to know more.

One strategy is to not give answers, but instead present questions, puzzles and challenges from which more questions will arise. Sending them out confused may sound counter intuitive, but it will ensure that they will want to find out more. Encouraging them to use the personal devices they are intimately familiar with to go and find the knowledge they are unfamiliar with is enquiry-based learning for the digital age. Their mobile phones are the tools they carry around with them, and they will undoubtedly use similar tools when they enter the world of work.

Personal mind tools will enable them to access content that will satisfy their curiosity, and will lead to them to discover even more questions. Enquiry through interaction with their digital world will mould them into independent learners in preparation for the challenging times ahead.

Breaking down the subject silos

Many schools lag woefully behind the current needs of society; for example, in the compartmentalisation of learning in subject silos. A 21st century curriculum would do away with such false boundaries. If all subjects have overlaps and commonalities, lessons should incorporate several subjects. Children need to understand these overlaps to obtain a clear and full picture of their world. Without a holistic curriculum, students find it difficult to make connections between science and maths, or understand how art and music have influenced history. Some schools – such as Albany Senior High School in Auckland, New Zealand – are already breaking down the subject silos and supporting learning spaces where students can switch quickly between subjects across the curriculum. We will discover more about this and several other innovative schools later in the book.

When I first published these arguments on my blog, they clearly touched a nerve. They were deliberately provocative, and as I had expected, attracted a storm of comments. Some were keenly supportive, others were antagonistic to my position, and there were one or two whose zealousness overcame them, causing them to 'play the man rather than the ball'. All sides fought their corners well, arguing from their respective stances on the fundamental nature and philosophy of knowledge, and the specific role that school plays in education. Some comments pointed out that resources, teacher styles, assessment methods and time were important factors in determining the relevance and efficacy of curricula in schools.

But – and here I will continue to be provocative – I feel that some commentators are missing the point completely, so I will reiterate my argument. The key point I am making is not that knowledge is bad. Clearly, the more we know and understand about our world, the better equipped we will be to meet as yet unforeseen challenges. My argument is that technology is our greatest ally in our attempts to keep that knowledge constantly updated and relevant. Furthermore, I believe that predominantly content-based curricula and the traditional compartmentalisation of subjects constrains student learning, and no longer prepares them sufficiently for a dynamic world of work that is in a constant state of change.

Today we have a vast array of technology at our fingertips, and – although this is seldom enough to make informed decisions and knowledgeable actions on its own – combined with the appropriate knowledge, skills and literacies, individuals will have the ability to apply creative solutions to problems they may encounter on a daily basis. Critical thinking, flexibility, working collaboratively, and creative problem solving are all key components for success in changing environments. But 'knowing that' and 'knowing how' will not be enough. Students also need to know why.

My approach to the reform of any school curriculum would therefore be to provide a fairer balance of declarative, procedural and critical skills that can be applied in pragmatic ways in constantly changing conditions. How we might achieve it is the subject of the next section.

Curriculum as conversation

In his 1996 book *Curriculum as Conversation*, Arthur Applebee[3] argued that much of the school curriculum of the time was based upon:

> ... false premises and reflects a fundamental misconception of the nature of knowing. They strip knowledge of the contexts that give it meaning and vitality, and lead to an education that stresses knowledge-out-of-context rather than knowledge-in-action. In such a system students are taught about the traditions of the past, and not how to enter into and participate in those of the present and the future.

It is clear that in the years since the book was first published, little has changed. Knowledge is still presented largely out of context, when it should and could be situated in authentic contexts. I have asked this question before, but I will ask it again.

Are we preparing students for the past, or for the future?

---

3 Arthur N. Applebee, *Curriculum as Conversation: Transforming Traditions of Teaching and Learning* (Chicago: University of Chicago Press, 1996), p. 3.

Situated learning

If we are interested in preparing students for the future, we need to understand that contexts are changing more rapidly than curricular content, and what is taught in schools can quickly become obsolete. We can therefore no longer afford to rely solely on content, and need to present more situated and authentic learning opportunities. Situated approaches to learning involve an emphasis on context as well as on content, and the best way to experience appropriate contexts is to 'do it for real', or in Applebee's terms, to experience it as knowledge-in-action. Sometimes this can be achieved through focused dialogue.

Carl Young[4] relates the story of a language teacher who used pure conversation as the basis for all her teaching. Although this sounds like an obvious method for language learning, which invariably has conversation at its heart, it is actually quite profound. It engages students, compelling them to draw on the knowledge they already possess, applying it in unfamiliar contexts, reflecting on their experiences, and emerging with new understanding. I propose that similar dialogic approaches can and should be applied to the teaching of all subjects across the curriculum.

Working a power shift

My former colleague Alan Bleakley[5] takes situated learning and equalising the role of the teacher further, arguing that much of formal education is sadly still based on power differentials between teacher and student, and calls for a more horizontal, democratised form of education where students have equal say in the process. Bleakley echoes the earlier work of Paulo Freire,[6] who pointed out the following:

---

4 Carl A. Young, 'Conversation as Curriculum: Learning to Teach English in Rural America', *English Journal* (2004): 82–88.
5 Alan Bleakley, 'Curriculum as Conversation', *Advances in Health Sciences Education* 14.3 (2009): 297–301.
6 Paulo Freire, *Pedagogy of the Oppressed* (London: Bloomsbury Publishing, 2000).

Education must begin with the solution of the teacher–student contradiction, by reconciling the poles of the contradiction so that both are simultaneously teachers and students.

Bleakley elaborates:

Democracy in education requires interplay between the individual and the collective through authentic dialogue – as the reconstructionists suggest, constructing curriculum as an extended and complicated conversation.

To achieve this requires teachers to assume a role as learners, while students are allowed to become teachers, to facilitate the free and open dialogue that will constitute conversation as curriculum. Freire argues that authentic thinking, that is thinking centred upon what is real, occurs regularly within run of the mill communication, but rarely anywhere in isolation. He advances this argument by asserting that if thought has deeper meaning when it derives from authentic actions in the real world, students cannot be dominated by their teachers, but both assume an equal status.

To achieve this kind of pedagogical equality, teachers will need a new mindset. There must be a power shift in the classroom where teachers transform their roles, moving from instructor to co-learner. Freire argues that we cannot engage in open dialogue if we lack humility, and that this kind of pedagogy will fail if we think we know it all and fail to acknowledge our own ignorance in certain areas. My students are surprised when I tell them that I would like to learn something from them, and at first they fail to grasp the implications. It is not an expression of weakness on the part of the educator, but a shrewd pedagogical decision that opens the door for students to discover more, and learn more deeply, about their subject. If they are required to teach, they need to know their topic thoroughly. No one knows everything, but everyone knows something. Learning together through co-construction of knowledge seems to be a far more honest approach to pedagogy.

Learning through dialogue

The teachers who have inspired me most are those who have been accessible rather than remote, personable instead of stand-offish, and knowledgeable without being arrogant. Most importantly, they conversed with me rather than lectured.

One of the lecturers in the first year of my undergraduate degree inspired me to learn more and to push myself to my limits to become more knowledgeable in my subject area.

Dr Ken Gale did this using nothing more than a whiteboard and pen, along with constant discussion and questioning. Ken has since become one of my valued colleagues. This kind of simple Socratic discourse[7] was deceptively powerful, did wonders for my self-esteem and piqued my appetite for more knowledge. There was no need for him to use any other visual aids or learning resources. Ken simply pointed us in the direction of relevant reading, and strategically slipped the names of key theorists into his discussions with us.

For me this was a skilful but relaxed and unobtrusive kind of pedagogy, involving every student in the room, debating, deliberating and generally exploring together the nuances and intricacies of our subject. There was no lecturing, and there were no absolutes. Just the inspiration of the discussion and the joy of knowing that you were going to leave the classroom with more questions than when you came in.

It seems clear to me that to encourage open and frank dialogue in a formal learning environment, the power differential between teacher and student must be removed. When teachers wish to promote democratic learning, students are given licence to challenge and are encouraged to discuss, debate and argue. Passive consumption of delivered knowledge is then replaced by full engagement with the subject matter through conversation. The conversation around the topic becomes the new curriculum, enabling each student to act as an open minded, independent thinker who can defend his or her position without resorting to dogmatic assertions based on partial understanding or incomplete knowledge. The best teachers encourage all students to participate

---

7   Paul Woodruff, 'Socratic Education', *Philosophers on Education*, 1998: 14–31.

and value all contributions, incorporating as many as possible into an extended conversation around the topic.

In the digital age, conversation as curriculum can be extended beyond the classroom into the use of social media and other communication technologies. Conversation for learning across a number of platforms suggests that two or more discussions can occur simultaneously. It may be impossible to change the curriculum we are tasked to deliver. However, teachers who appreciate the merits of conversation in a truly Socratic mode will redesign lessons to incorporate learning activities to reflect it.

Learning by making

Let me give you an example of how this works in practice. Back in the early nineties, when I was working in nurse education, I introduced a project where students were given an entire day to create a five-minute video on a subject directly related to their course. In groups of threes and fours, the student nurses were sent out to conceive their video, script and storyboard it, decide on roles, procure their props, scout out shooting locations, record their video, and then edit it. Then, during the final hour of the day, each group introduced, presented and discussed their five-minute video.

Some of my colleagues were sceptical about the value of this kind of approach to learning. They argued that it was a waste of time when the nurses could be studying their textbooks, writing their essays, or practising how to give injections to oranges. I countered that the students were, in fact, engaged in a very high level of cognitive activity where they were engaged in learning by making.

It wasn't until a few years later when I discovered the work of Seymour Papert that I was able to build a theoretical framework around the nurses' video projects. In his theory of constructionism, Papert[8] argued that we build mental representations of what we learn, and that the situated nature of where we learn influences and strengthens that representation. In other words, we learn by doing

---

8   Seymour Papert, *Mindstorms: Children, Computers and Powerful Ideas* (Brighton: Harvester Press, 1980).

and building within relevant environments, and that authentic tasks can be very powerful in support of that situated learning.

At the time I showed my colleagues that the student nurses were learning numerous skills that they would later be able to transfer across into their professional practice. To successfully complete their video project they needed to be able to solve problems, create content, construct artefacts, make decisions and make critical judgements, work together as a team, divide their labour and select appropriate tasks, manage their time, think creatively, negotiate difficult situations, consider ethical issues, work with finite resources, successfully bring a task to completion and reflect on their practice.

How many of these skills could be modelled and situated within a classroom in such a short period of time? The very act of constructing something tangible allows students to test out hypotheses, learn from each other and solve problems as they progress. Learning by making causes abstract ideas and concepts to become concrete because they are situated in real life contexts.

These are essential skills for 21st century working. It is for these reasons that making things is a central part of all my courses, whether it is a video, podcast, blog or any other digital artefact. In so doing students are constructing their own versions of knowledge, gaining a sense of ownership and investing their energies and their ingenuity in making and presenting it.

Students are doing it for themselves

For the longest time, teachers and lecturers have held the monopoly on the production of academic content. They create schemes of work and lesson plans, produce resources, devise marking schemes and search around for activities and games they can repurpose to use in teaching sessions. It's very hard work, but there is a better way – encourage students to do it themselves.

Although the production of content has been the preserve of the teacher and academic since the formalisation of education, increasingly now we see learners creating their own content. They have the tools, they own the technology, and they have the confidence to use them, not only informally, but increasingly within formal learning contexts too. Many are prolific and proficient in producing blogs, podcasts, videos and photos for sharing on the Web. They can do all of this using the small smartphone in their pocket.

This user-generated content trend is becoming apparent not only in universities and colleges but also in the compulsory education sectors.

What are the implications of this trend? There are many, but in this chapter I will highlight just five key areas educators need to consider.

Changing teacher roles

Firstly, the traditional role of teachers is changing. The good news is that teachers will not be redundant in the new technology-rich learning economy. However, they will need to adapt as conditions change, becoming guides and mentors rather than instructors. As teachers switch from directors to co-producers, from pedagogues to co-learners, they will begin to discover the power of peer production, and the deeper engagement students can achieve when they research and learn for themselves. I believe this shift was going to happen anyway, even before learners started to create their own content.

Teacher roles have been moving from didactic to facilitative roles ever since constructivist theories started to enter into teacher training curricula.

Student-centred learning

Secondly, partly as a result of the first trend, learners are becoming more central to the learning process. Where once students were seen as the passive recipients and end products of schooling, now they are an integral part of the learning process and play an active role in their own education. Students are assuming greater responsibility for their own learning, and in so doing, are gaining greater insights into the process of learning by creating their own content around their studies.

Personalised learning and the student experience are written large into the mission statements of many leading universities worldwide. University leaders are waking up to the fact that students are now customers who need to be heard. Consequently, learners now have a voice in the affairs of many institutions, and are playing an increasingly active part in the governance of many programmes of study. It's not simply about having a say, however. Students are also deciding the pace and place of their learning. As we will see in a later chapter in this book, learners now have the tools to learn independently, on the move, at times and in places that suit their lifestyles.

Student-centred learning is clearly where education providers recognise they should locate themselves. Teachers now need to wake up to the fact that they don't teach subjects, they teach people.

Learners as producers

Thirdly, content becomes more engaging because students invest their own time, energy and vision into creating it. They gain personal ownership over their learning. They place their own individual stamp on the content they create, and then share it within their personal learning environment and across their peer network. Thereby, in gaining an audience for their content, they are spurred on further to develop, refine and perfect not only their content but, indirectly and probably unwittingly, their understanding of the knowledge their content represents. There is little more motivating than a receptive audience that appreciates your knowledge and skills. Social media tools such as blogs and video sharing sites facilitate this process, but they do so on a global scale.

Fourthly, students are becoming evaluators as well as producers of learning content. Because they produce content, they also tend to consume existing content to help them create their own work. This puts them in an ideal position to assess the quality, relevance and provenance of the content they encounter. In so doing, they are acquiring and practising some of the key digital literacies they will need later in their careers.

Also, many learners find out how to produce their content to an acceptable standard by evaluating other people's content, and although useful guidance can come from experts such as teachers and lecturers, autodidacticism is increasingly taking a central place in the student experience.

Finally, the context in which the content is produced is assuming more importance. The importance of the situatedness of learning at all levels cannot be overemphasised. Some of the strongest experiences and lessons we learn are rooted in authentic contexts, cultures and activities. In work-based learning this is particularly vital, as it enables workers to embed themselves within their work culture and learn more deeply about the social, political, technical and economic contexts that are specific to their employment.

Some readers may argue that this is an idealistic position to adopt regarding self-learning and user-generated content. My response would be – look around you and see what is happening inside and outside of the classroom. Learners tend to be more resilient and able than many teachers give them credit for. They have unprecedented access to a large array of new technologies, connecting and communicating in ways previous generations could only imagine.

Most importantly, creating, repurposing, organising and sharing content are a way of life for this generation. They are identified, and maintain their identities, through their presence on social media and are very familiar with the terrain. Schools, colleges and universities that support the ethos of student-generated content will find themselves tapping directly into the rich mother lode of creativity and innovation this generation of learners offers.

7

New Learning Architectures

Each new situation requires a new architecture.

Jean Nouvel

Where is the front?

In school I was always told to face the front, stay in my seat and pay attention to my teacher. You see, the front was where the teacher was, where the blackboard was located, and the front was ostensibly where all the action was. Learning whilst facing the front was supposed to make me more attentive, focus my mind, enable me to grasp what the teacher was saying, and make it easier for me to memorise the facts. I was a recipient of the educational culture of the day, and what I was essentially going through was a 'mug and jug' kind of education.

I was the empty mug that needed to be filled. My teacher was the jug – filled to brimming with knowledge which s/he imparted by pouring it into me. If I attained a high enough set of grades from my exams, I was deemed a good student.

Yet, in the sage words of the poet William Butler Yeats, 'Education is not the filling of a pail, but the lighting of a fire.' This is the true essence of engagement. It's a shame that I, along with many other children, was forced by my school to be a pail.

Later that academic year, I was expected to sit down, again facing the front, and spell out everything I had memorised in a form that was acceptable to the examiners before I was allowed to progress to the next stage of my instruction. But facing the front didn't work for me. I was too easily distracted by the butterfly outside the classroom window, or the jet aircraft screaming by overhead. I was too interested in catching the eye of the pretty girl sitting across the room from me, or the card games that were going on under the tables next to me. Instead of taking notes, I was more intent on creating cartoon characters, writing stories and poems and drawing fantastic scenes in my exercise books.

I was also a fidget. I didn't want to stay still in my uncomfortable chair, facing constantly in one direction. It simply wasn't in my nature. I wanted to move around and face other directions, because in doing so I was less bored, I could see and interact with the rest of my classmates, and it gave me much more freedom to explore what I was learning, to experiment, to ask the 'what if' questions, and to take risks.

I liked walking around as I was learning. My teachers frowned upon this, and insisted that if I couldn't stay in my seat and face the front, I would be punished. Punishment in those days was something to be feared – the cane (in my English school) or the strap (in my Scottish school). So I reluctantly sat and faced the front, and became more and more bored and frustrated with school and sadly, more disenchanted with learning.

School was something to endure rather than enjoy.

Switching on to learning

It was only later, when I left school and began my career, that I eventually became switched on to learning and began to enjoy formal study. It took me many years to shake out of the school-induced learning lethargy.

One teacher who did inspire me in my final two years at school was a liberal-minded American music and drama teacher by the name of Larry Domaigne. In those days, the curriculum was gender biased. It was an unfair situation for all. Boys were required to study all the sciences – chemistry, physics and biology – but girls were only allowed to choose one. Conversely, girls could opt to study home economics, art and music, while boys could only study one of those subjects. I loved art and music and I excelled in both. I hated physical education, which was timetabled at the same time as music, and so for my final school year, I absented myself from PE and sat in the back of Larry Domaigne's class. He knew my game, knew I was breaking the rules, but he turned a blind eye and no one ever stopped me. Larry inspired me to be different, to take risks, and to appreciate learning for the sake of learning, not because of the subject matter. He had such an enthusiasm for his subject, and he had an incredible passion for conveying this to his students. I learnt a lot about performance, staging and composing from his lessons, and also participated in the extra-curricular activities, such as the plays and musicals he organised and the lunchtime impromptu concerts that were held in the music room. Although I was never destined to become a professional musician or actor, the time spent in his class taught me more about myself than I learnt in any other class that year. I also like to think that I picked up several skills that would later transfer into my career as an educator and public speaker. It was the beginnings of my awakening into what learning was really all about. It was a shame that it only happened in my final school year.

I was in my late thirties when I successfully completed my first degree in psychology with first class honours. I studied part-time through the British Open University, while holding down a full-time job and a part-time evening teaching job at the local college. I managed to complete my degree in three years, something I was warned simply 'could not be done'. When someone tells me something can't be done, I'll do it anyway to prove them wrong. I achieved my degree because I was interested, had discovered my own creative and intellectual abilities, and was able to think for myself. It was learning in my own time, in my own space, and it was self-regulated. I could move around while I studied, and my learning was my own responsibility. I had found my own 'front' to face.

It was the most liberating experience of my life. I wonder how much more success we would see in our schools if we provided environments where our students could discover their own creative and intellectual capabilities, and were given the freedom to express them?

As Richard Merrick[1] recently observed, 'People need to change. Organisations don't.' And there's the rub – schools, colleges and universities are organisations that change very slowly if they change at all, but the people in them, the teachers, lecturers and professors,

---

1 Richard Merrick, 'Choose Your Own Flight Path', Inspiration Engineering, 16 July, 2011. Available online at: http://inspirationengineering. com/2011/07/16/534/.

do need to change. Teachers and learners need to find their own front to face.

We need to realise that everything we do changes the structure of our brains, and that also applies to our students. New connections are made with each new item of knowledge, and learning is a limitless process. We need to encourage our students to do things and experience things that change the structures of their brains positively. Teachers who believe in personalised learning should avoid imposing the 'face the front' regime which is largely responsible for conditioning learners to blindly obey the rules, submit to the status quo without question, and follow instructions rather than thinking for themselves. I strongly believe we should move away from the ludicrous idea that 'one size fits all' and the tyranny of homogeneity. It makes sense that educators should provide latitude for creative freedom and room for individual expression in the classroom.

We should give students the space to decide for themselves which direction they wish to face.

Being a learning architect

I hope I have convinced you that in formal education contexts, such as school, the space in which students learn is important. It's not simply about inspiration. If the design of a space is wrong, learning can be constrained or even completely stifled. It's hard to engage students when their surroundings are poor. Too much noise, not enough light, too much heat or cold, uncomfortable seats, even poorly configured seating in a classroom can adversely affect learning.

Teachers should be the architects of learning spaces.

I remember the dire environment that I endured as a pupil in one unfortunate primary school. This was in the early sixties, when scant attention was paid to the design of learning spaces. The classroom had bare floorboards and dingy walls, and the desk and chair sets were fixed to the floor. The classroom and the corridors echoed with every footstep, and there was no heating. All we had was one fireplace which was never lit, due to 'health and safety' issues.

The toilets were located in a block across the concrete playground, and we avoided going there because they were exposed to the elements; the toilet block was cold and dark, and we knew that spiders lurked. We very quickly learnt not to drink at all during the school day so we wouldn't need to negotiate our way across the courtyard to the toilets. We were often cold and thirsty because of our learning environment. Naturally, it didn't lead to very good learning outcomes.

Attention to detail

Simple things often make all the difference. Recent research has shown that drinking water regularly actually improves concentration and focus. It's often the prosaic things that improve the learning environment, and as blogger Stephen Heppell has remarked, better school toilets equal better results.

When I state that teachers should be architects of learning spaces, I mean they should seriously consider the spaces within which students learn. It's not just about giving students more freedom to learn. If necessary, teachers should be prepared to step in and redesign their classroom spaces. The simple, everyday things are important in the design of learning spaces.

Equally important as a design consideration is the way technology is embedded into the learning environment. There have been many discussions on how best to deploy technology in schools. Embedding computers into the curriculum is one thing. Deploying them effectively within the physical confines of a school is another matter entirely. If teachers establish a computer lab or ICT suite, all of the technology is contained within one space. This may sound sensible, but a message is sent to the students that 'this is the place where computing is done'.

In an age where computing can be done in the palm of your hand or on your lap, wherever you are, this is not the best message to send. On the other hand, a school-wide implementation of Wi-Fi connectivity to support the use of laptops or handhelds also presents its own problems.

The following is an excerpt from a fictional account I wrote in which a school leader is describing the problems she encountered when she attempted to introduce new technology into her school:

A Head Teacher Writes...

We have had pencils in our school now for some time, and we were one of the first to adopt them, but it has been an uphill struggle. There aren't enough to go around, and often several of the children have to crowd around to use the pencils at the same time. But we are better off than many schools. We have a well-equipped pencil suite where the chained desktop pencils are used in special sessions, and often, as a reward for good behaviour, children are allowed to come into the suite (under teacher supervision, of course) to use the pencils to draw fun things.

Pencils were resisted by some of the teachers at first, because they complained they would have to change their practice if they adopted them. And they were right: pencils are in fact a game changer. Others were worried that they would not have enough time to learn to use them properly.

I have a wider vision than a pencil suite for our school. I'm considered a bit of a maverick and many of my staff look at me and shake their heads sadly. You see, I have a vision for pencils that I think will transform our school and enhance learning for all our students. Wait for it – I am advocating one pencil for every child in the school! And even more radical than that, I want to introduce pencils that can be used by students while they are on the move. Yes, I know it sounds absurd, but I think it will work. Needless to say, I have had many objections and lots of opposition from all quarters.

Some teachers, led by our school pencil co-ordinator, have complained that we made a considerable investment in the pencil suite, and it's being used regularly for very important teaching. OK, so there is only one pencil between every four children, but at least the pencils are being used consistently, she argues. Some occasionally break and have to be sent away to be fixed, but we also have a parent who is familiar with pencils, and has one at home. He comes in occasionally to fix them, which saves us some money.

My idea is for the school to invest more money so that each child can walk around while using their pencils, and that they can even take them home with them! Yes, I know it's an extremely radical idea, and that's the very reason I am receiving so much opposition. Some of my teaching staff are arguing that we could better spend the money on more chalk for the blackboards. Others are warning that children will either damage the pencils or worse, lose them if they take them out of school. Pencils are meant to be used for education, they say, not for fun.

Even the parents are complaining. Some have written a very strong letter to the governors, suggesting that if we give a pencil to each of the children to bring home they will need to revise their home contents insurance, in case any disaster occurs and the child damages the pencil in some way. Some of the richer families don't seem to mind, as they have better pencils at home than we could possibly buy for the school. It's a kind of pencil envy I suppose. There does seem to be a pencil divide across the local community.

I am confident though that giving one pencil to each student will address this problem.

Then there are the objections from the TaxPayers' Alliance and other pressure groups who have even gone onto the local TV station to complain that we are being irresponsible, and are wasting valuable taxpayers' money on purchasing a pencil for every child. 'In my day,' said the TPA spokesperson, 'we used slates and styluses and shared them around, and we were happy. One pencil per child is simply a gimmick.' To be blunt, I think they are missing the point. I strongly believe that pencils are the future of learning, and the less tethered they are, the greater the flexibility of learning for all subjects across the curriculum.

One of the strongest arguments from some of my teaching staff is that they claim to be pencil immigrants, while the children are pencil natives. The kids seem to have such an affinity with the pencils, whilst the teaching staff struggle to use them and get embarrassed when they accidentally use the wrong end, or the point is blunt and they don't know how to sharpen it. Some teachers have warned that increased use of the pencil can be addictive, and will cause all sorts of problems such as writer's cramp, eye strain, raised incidences of graffiti in the school toilets and rude cartoons of teachers passed around the room. Such dangers though are far outweighed by the benefits of mobile, personalised pencils.

So we will forge on with my new one child, one pencil scheme, and as a school we will make it work. We will actually purchase the new second-generation (2G) pencils, which have erasers attached, and in so doing, these multi-functional tools will offer a revolutionary approach to learning. They are also much faster and last longer than the old pencils.

> I will close with this inspirational quote: 'Any teacher who can be replaced by a pencil ... should be!' – Arthur C. Chalk

The above passage was obviously intended as a parody, with the simple word substitution of pencil for computer. The humour lies in the absurdity of the head teacher's predicament. And yet computers and pencils are both technologies, and both, when introduced into conservative environments in their respective eras, made people anxious and provoked significant resistance.

New designs for learning

I have been keenly interested in the design of learning spaces for some time. My early background was as a designer – I attended Hereford College of Art and Design in the seventies, where I studied fine art and eventually, graphic design. My more recent professional life as an educator has drawn me back to this again and again. I'm very fortunate to be able to travel around the world and visit schools, colleges and universities in many different countries. Each is different, because places of learning should reflect the cultures of those who use them.

Academic grafitti

The design of learning spaces does not have to be complicated. Not all successful solutions have to be high tech or high cost. Just as impressive for me are the spaces I have seen in non-technology focused 'chill out' rooms, both at the University of Queensland in Brisbane, Australia and at the University College of St Mark and St John in Plymouth, England. The walls and doors and many other surfaces in these rooms are made of material that can be written on with dry-wipe markers. Similar to whiteboard surfaces, these spaces can be used by students for creating mind-maps, flowcharts, diagrams, brainstorming lists – in fact just about anything that helps them to learn better. The students love it because they can then capture their images with a mobile phone for later use. It's academic graffiti. It's a simple, cost effective idea that to my surprise has not been taken up by other institutions on a grander scale.

The same concept is appearing in schools, according to Stephen Heppell. In his Pinterest collection of Good Tested Ideas,[2] he features a school that has adopted the idea of writing surfaces for its students' desktops. Back in the days when I was at school we had wooden desktops, and I remember writing my name (and several other things which I won't repeat here) onto my desktop in ink. Some went further and carved their names more or less permanently into their desks. We often got into trouble, but we were simply making our mark. It was the classroom version of carving our names into the bark of a tree. Young people seem to have an innate need to make their mark, to tag, to create graffiti – and often schools are fighting a losing battle trying to stop them from making their mark somewhere in the school – on their desks, the walls, the doors or windows. What better way to capture that natural energy and channel it creatively than to provide children with wipeable surfaces they can use to help them with their learning? Creative surfaces will mean that 'making your mark' will take on an entirely new meaning.

Shared spaces and joined-up thinking

Another place of learning I was privileged to visit was Albany Senior High School in North Auckland, New Zealand where I was invited to talk to a group of educators gathered from across the city. I was shown around the school prior to my presentation.

The vision statement of the school was simple but powerful: *We nurture each other, we inspire each other, we empower each other.*

Entering the reception area of ASHS via the lift, I encountered a cafeteria area similar to any found in the corporate world. The school's deputy principal told me: 'We offer the students an environment where they are treated like adults. When they are dealt with in this way, they take on adult responsibilities and behaviour.' Moving through from the reception into the main school, it was evident that open plan, flexible spaces were the key design feature, and personalised learning the norm. Students were sitting in areas where they could interact with each other and the teachers, and

---

2 Stephen Heppell, 'Good Tested Ideas to Transform Learning' (2014). Available online at: http://www.pinterest.com/stephenheppell/good-tested-ideas-to-transform-learning/.

there could be up to three separate classes taking place in the same space, with students able to move around the room and across the curricular topics seamlessly. Gone was the silo mentality of 'now you are in a science class'.

A central tenet of the school's curriculum delivery is that students know why they are learning something new, and can then connect it to real life contexts.

Mixing it up

When I visited Skipton Girls School in Yorkshire, England, my eyes were opened again to other possibilities. Skipton Girls School is a rarity in education, being one of a very small number of designated engineering colleges for girls. The subject silos have disappeared here too as the students also learn several subjects in combination. The school leadership sees no separation between subjects, preferring to conceive them all as connected, and this was particularly evident in its impact when I spoke to the children. Learning through enquiry- and project-based education are central to the school's strategy.

One group showed me their physics and music project, in which they were designing and experimenting with synthesisers. They proudly demonstrated how they could change frequencies to create waveforms and produce new sounds. They had already made the connections between the wiggly lines on the screen and the sound they could make, and more importantly, they had learnt that there is a cause and effect. Change the waveform shape and the sound also changes. This was a part of the curriculum that was unwritten, but still incredibly powerful. In one of my final conversations at the school, I asked one of the students why she thought it was important to learn subjects together rather than separately.

She thought for a minute and then said: 'Because it helps me to understand the world better.'

Opening up education

It was refreshing to see that some schools also advocate the use of open source software. The deputy principal at ASHS told me that in his school they also practice a Bring Your Own Device (BYOD) option for all its students. He argued that the most equitable way to avoid any digital divides is to provide open source software to all students. If they own no device of their own, there are computers available in all the learning spaces. I was impressed with the fully equipped dance studio and next door, another studio for audio and video projects, complete with a green screen room. ASHS even has its own YouTube channel.

The visionary principal sees her school as one of many that will emerge in the next few years across the region. She told me that the 800 or so students have over 50 teaching staff to support them. That, by any estimation, is a great student to teacher ratio. The free, open, flexible spaces and the policy of BYOD ensure that the school is both an attractive and sustainable place to learn. Furthermore, all the resources the teachers create for teaching and assessment are licensed under Creative Commons for free use by other educators. My hope is that we will see other schools using this model in the future, not only in New Zealand, but further afield.

Fabulous learning spaces

I once heard Stephen Heppell talk about another version of combining classes together. In 'Super Classes' three classes are joined together for one lesson, and the three teachers team teach. The lead teacher (or narrator) is responsible for conducting the session, whilst teacher 2 (the 'breakdown engineer') offers the intervention when students are struggling, and teacher 3 provides differentiated intervention for those learners who require it. This might mean, for example, intervening to support a student with special needs in a specific task. Conducting classes in this way drives the session forward with fewer stops and starts. Teachers can focus on their individual roles and in so doing maintain the impetus of the lesson without being sidetracked to respond to the needs of individual learners.

It's not just the shape of the learning space that is important, sometimes it's the concept. In Australia, Stephen Harris, principal of the Sydney Centre for Innovation in Learning (SCIL) has devised a range of metaphors that describe different kinds of activities that might take place in shared learning spaces. The space and activity juxtapositions at SCIL rely extensively on each teacher's willingness to be flexible and adaptable to change and responsive to learner needs as they arise, and also to tap into the huge potential of young people's innate ability to be agile and adept at using new technologies. Names such as the 'camp fire' and the 'watering hole' connote a variety of activities the students can own and occupy. The 'camp fire' is clearly a place where stories can be told, whilst the 'watering hole' connotes a place of refreshment where learners can relax and 'chill out' for a while. The technology travels with them as they move around within these spaces.

Schools are often designed by architects and designers who may have spent little time in school since their childhood days. The best schools of the digital age are those that are designed by people who understand the learning process, and can incorporate the best new technologies in those spaces. Getting those who actually use the school every week – the students – to design them in conjunction with their teachers seems to be a dynamic strategy and might lead to even better creative learning spaces.

It's clear that learning spaces are a vitally important component of the school to get right. If we don't provide the best possible spaces, that are conducive to learning, we are letting the children down. It's not just what we provide in schools that makes a difference, but how we provide it.

Technology Enhanced Active Learning environments

In the digital age, the boundaries of informal and formal spaces have blurred significantly, as have the boundaries between the real and the virtual. It is becoming increasingly less important where learning occurs, as long as it is meaningful learning. Some might argue that learning that is situated is the most meaningful and therefore the most powerful. It is also important that learning is made to be active and engaging. If any of these components is missing, then clearly learning has not been optimised.

When children learn, they do so through interaction with others, observation and practice, discovery and experimentation and by doing and making. All of these aspects of learning are active. When they enter into formal education, they enter into an artificial environment where learning is managed, directed and organised for them.

It is not hard then to see how such an artificial transition from active to passive can stifle creativity and demotivate learners.

As a response to the problems of learning in homogenised, regimented environments such as classrooms and lecture halls, Technology Enhanced Active Learning (TEAL) came into being. TEAL is one of several approaches to moving away from tedious, passive learning environments where students are expected to listen, take laborious notes and memorise what is being said and presented. TEAL spaces feature several characteristics, including flexible learning spaces where furniture can be moved into many alternative configurations, technology enriched contexts (wireless and untethered, Web enabled and personal technologies) and a shift from teacher led lessons to student-centred learning, where the learner can take control and the teacher is there to facilitate. The techno-romantic argument is that simply having access to personalised technologies creates conducive conditions in which active learning can occur.

More pragmatically, we see the role of the teacher is also paramount to the success of TEAL approaches. Without strategic input from teachers at critical junctures during a lesson, and without some clear goal or set of objectives, students can lose focus, become distracted and go off task.

The idea that students should be able to move freely around the learning space whilst remaining connected is a powerful one, as has already been outlined above. The possibilities of learning through collaboration with other students and the potential to manage their own pace of learning are also very powerful. Students who can connect to online resources, social spaces and content also have freedom not only to search and discover, but also to create, revise and share their own content.

A number of psychological and social learning theories can be applied to explain the transformative potential of this approach. These include not only the Zone of Proximal Development[3] and scaffolding[4] but also social modelling[5] and social comparison theory.[6] The latter two may come into play where learners see the success of other learners and modify their own approaches to optimise the best and most active aspects of their own learning.

S'cool Radio

Westfields Junior School in Hampshire, England, has reported great learning results through activities supported by the use of games, mobile technology, video, music technology and other specialised software. One great innovative idea head teacher Karine George told me about was particularly useful for engaging children across the entire curriculum. Their learning activities are scaffolded through their own Internet radio channel: S'cool Radio.

The children take turns in operating and hosting the radio channel, working in pairs. They take the responsibility of writing and producing their own shows, and in doing so they are able to reach out not only to their own peers (the radio shows are broadcast over public address systems during break times) and their parents, but also the wider community, and ultimately, to a worldwide audience.

Other schools also do this, to engage their children in learning a range of skills and discrete sets of knowledge that can be more or less instantly 'performed' to an audience.

---

3 Lev Vygotsky, *Mind in Society: The Development of Higher Psychological Processes* (Cambride MA: Harvard University Press, 1980).

4 Jerome S. Bruner, *Actual Minds, Possible Worlds* (Cambridge MA: Harvard University Press, 2009).

5 Albert Bandura, 'Social Learning' in Antony S. R. Manstead and Miles Hewstone (eds.) *The Blackwell Encyclopedia of Social Psychology* (Blackwell Publishing, 1999): 576–581.

6 Leon Festinger, 'A Theory of Social Comparison Processes', *Human Relations* 7.2 (1954): 117–140.

The hidden audience effect

In effect, S'cool Radio takes a similar approach to Dave Mitchell's QuadBlogging concept but develops it using other media. What both projects have in common is their use of the 'hidden audience' effect. Dave Mitchell stresses the importance of providing an audience for young bloggers, who then 'perform' their ideas and writing skills, receiving feedback from their peers. It is highly motivational to know you have an audience. Performance levels are raised as extra effort is made. The meteoric success of QuadBlogging lies in its organisation of four school clusters, which provide a guaranteed audience to read and comment on every post the children make.

Evidence from earlier studies I conducted with my own research team in Plymouth in 2007 revealed that the hidden audience who read my students' wiki content encouraged them to raise their game in terms of improved academic writing, greater accuracy, deeper critical analysis and thinking, and a more polished presentation style. The entire account of that research can be found in my article 'The Good, the Bad and the Wiki'.[7]

Clearly, the hidden audience effect is only one of the components that make projects such as QuadBlogging and S'cool Radio a success. For Westfields Junior children, the ability to communicate clearly, self-organise, self-broadcast, express ideas, work in a team, problem solve, plan ahead and think on one's feet are all brought into play when they plan, present and perform their Internet radio shows. The Westfields Internet radio project is therefore destined to be a great success, because not only does it provide learners with a ready-made audience, it also gives them space to practise and acquire these key transferable skills. These are skills they will certainly need to use when they enter a world of work that is uncertain and in a constant state of change.

---

7   Steve Wheeler, Peter Yeomans and Dawn Wheeler, 'The Good, the Bad and the Wiki: Evaluating student-generated content for collaborative learning', *British Journal of Educational Technology* 39.6 (2008): 987–995.

Pigcams and eggcams

My wife, Dawn Wheeler, is a teacher of English at a large community college just across the river from our Plymouth home. Several years ago, under the outstanding leadership of deputy head teacher Dan Roberts, Saltash.net set up a very innovative learning environment within its grounds. Teachers created a small working farm in the middle of the large secondary school, where the students were able to keep pigs, goats and chickens. The children took turns in caring for the animals, buying food, selling produce and generally managing the farm. During this time, teachers at the school found many ingenious ways to use the farm to enhance children's learning experiences.

The school installed a webcam in the chicken coop. Known as the 'eggcam', the camera streamed live video to the world through the school's website. Later in the project, a 'pigcam' in the pig sty webcasted the birth of piglets to a fascinated global audience, attracting in excess of 100,000 views in a single 24-hour period.

The students wrote blogs and made videos and podcasts about the farm animals, and showcased their work on the Saltash.net website. Large audiences viewed and commented on their work. Subsequently, the students were inspired to write more creatively and critically, thereby raising their attainment levels in literacy.

Numeracy skills were also positively impacted by the Saltash.net farm project. Being taught how to use a spreadsheet without a context can be a soulless experience. Needing to learn how to use a spreadsheet because you are required to demonstrate profit margins when you sell eggs at the market situates that learning and makes it more relevant and therefore more powerful.

Clearly, the use of space within schools is vital as the design of the learning environment can enhance learning or inhibit it. The manner in which technology is embedded within the learning space is also critical. Ensuring that situated forms of learning are supported will be one of the key concerns of educators in the coming years.

Equally important will be the opportunities schools provide for students to personalise their learning. That is the topic of the next chapter.

8
Making Learning Personal

Today you are you, that is truer than true. There is no one alive who is youer than you.

Theodor Geisel (Dr. Seuss)

Every person is a unique individual. Each shares views in common with their peers, but ultimately each learner experiences the world in an idiosyncratic way, and each brings his or her uniqueness into every situation they encounter. Clearly, one size does not fit all, and schools need to make provision for diversity at all levels. As we have already seen, most schools still operate on the basis of the factory model, which means individuals are often overlooked and their personal preferences are subsumed into the general day-to-day business of the school. Now we are in the digital age, schools have unprecedented opportunities to create improved learning experiences that place individual students at the heart of the process.

Students can, and do, create their own personalised learning. In earlier chapters I offered evidence that learning communities informally decide their own priorities. These can be observed in the folksonomies that emerge when digital content is organised, shared and curated. These processes occur in spite of the strictures and rules imposed upon students by their institutions. Most of the emergent properties of personal learning emanate from informal learning contexts, achieved outside and beyond the walls of the traditional education environment.

Desire lines

Should schools attempt to create personalised pathways for their students? Often, the answer is not to create pathways but instead to provide latitude for students to create their own. I recently heard a very good story about the building of a new university campus. Unusually, the architect hadn't designed any pedestrian paths into his plan. When asked why there were no pathways between the buildings, he replied cryptically that he was waiting to see what happened. Over a period of time, as students and staff walked between the buildings, they soon made their own tracks or 'desire lines' through the grass.

Once these tracks had become established as the most natural and preferred routes, the architect ordered the builders in to pave over the tracks. 'Better they create their own pathways,' he said, 'than for me to build them, and then for them not to be used.'

Instead of dogmatically imposing his own ideas onto the community, the architect had crowd-sourced his design.

Self-determined learning pathways are crucial for individual learners as well as learning communities and they are by their very nature beyond the control of universities and schools. Schools and universities cannot (and should not attempt to) harness these processes, but they can facilitate them. Just like the architect, institutions can refrain from imposing structures and pre-determined tools, wait to see what their students prefer and then provide them with the best possible conditions to support self-determined learning.

How often do we impose pathways upon students which do not meet their needs, or fail to fit their expectations? In earlier chapters of this book we discussed the issues surrounding current state-funded schooling. One of the questions raised was about poor planning and unwise investment in technology. We could, of course, make the same arguments about the building of new environments and curricula. If such decisions are ill-conceived, questions would be raised over whether they are simply a waste of time and resources. The institutional learning platform – the Virtual Learning Environment (VLE) or Learning Management System (LMS) – is a classic case of decisions being made about learning without consulting the learner, or indeed, even the practitioner.

There has been considerable debate since the inception of the VLE/LMS. The argument offered by those opposed to this approach is that when content is placed in a secure environment and is protected by passwords, it creates barriers to learning. Anyone who tries to enclose a network is doing it wrong. Closed networks limit communication, while open networks are powerful. Not only do VLEs restrict access, they can also restrict content. The architecture of the standard VLE/LMS requires that knowledge is offered in a homogenised format, and there is little space for personalisation of content. It offers students no possibilities of customising their experience inside the VLE/LMS and the design of the user interface is overcomplicated.

Subsequently, students and teachers find it very difficult to navigate their way through the system. The end result is that students spend more time thinking about which link to click next than they do about learning. They use the system only when they have to, but they use their personalised spaces such as their social media and networks when they want to. How can we reach a place in education where students find their own level and make their own pathways through learning?

One answer might lie in personal learning environments.

Personal learning environments

Originally intended as a counterpoint to the institutional Managed Learning Environment (iMLE), personal learning environments (PLEs) are now a much talked about concept in education. PLEs do exactly what they say on the can. They are different for each individual: created by them, owned by them, and used by them to support their lifelong learning. Much personal learning is informal, conducted in an unplanned manner throughout the day. PLEs are the basis for this kind of learning, supporting students' formal education while proffering opportunities for them to create new pathways to independent learning.

Ownership of such personal tools can be a bone of contention. Those involved in discussing technology-supported learning often cannot agree whether PLEs should remain the sole domain of the learner, or whether in some way they might be incorporated into institutional infrastructures. Some argue for sole student ownership of PLEs, vehemently opposed to any institutional interference; others hold the position that PLEs should have some institutional provision incorporated within them. Still others believe that PLEs should be part of the institutional infrastructure, brought within the protective envelope of the university firewall. Many locate themselves in middle-ground positions.

One important instance of this debate is the e-portfolio. Although a personal record of achievement and unique to each student, many e-portfolios sit within the confines of the institutional VLE.

My personal view is that students own and create their PLE but that the iMLE also has something useful to offer them, even though it is highly problematic in its current form. In my own experience, I see many students avoiding the iMLE because they either find it difficult to use or irrelevant to their daily learning. iMLEs are institutionally owned and are therefore managed by the institution. Often they become dumping grounds for content, are used unimaginatively by academic staff to pass messages on to groups of students, and if used to replicate instructional practices, can militate against good learning rather than encouraging it. Their poor design and navigation issues cause much frustration for students and teachers alike, leading to a general unpopularity of the system.

In short, many students prefer their own personal tools and will only use the institutional system when they really have to. It is a clash of concepts – no bridge seems possible, and the problem appears to be intractable.

I have been involved in several key debates over the last few years regarding these issues. I have played devil's advocate to promote discussion, engaging fruitfully with many knowledgeable peers. In the past I have argued provocatively that institutional VLEs present a number of problems for individual learners, not least the walled garden effect, which presents a great barrier to student freedom and creativity. Below is a tongue-in-cheek blog post which provoked some useful debate around the tensions between the PLE and the iMLE. In this piece I tried to capture the key arguments in an analogy with the Battle of Agincourt:

The two fingered salute

They stood facing each other across a muddy ploughed field. It had rained heavily the night before. On one side, flying their colourful banners, were the pride of French medieval nobility: at least 30,000 men in shining armour, armed to the teeth and ready for an overwhelming victory. On the other side, the army of Henry V, were less than 8,000 English and Welsh soldiers, weakened and bedraggled from weeks of forced marching, dysentery and hunger. The French looked like they had just stepped out of a Louis Vuitton boutique, and their opponents looked like crap. Yet over the course of a few hours, Henry's small dishevelled army systematically took their enemies to pieces with the result that the French dead were piled up in walls, and their noble families, sometimes three complete generations, were slaughtered like cattle.

The French snatched defeat from the jaws of victory, losing over 5,000 men while Henry's army sustained around 200 dead. The year was 1415, and the battle took place just outside the tiny French village of Azincourt (then Agincourt). The Battle of Agincourt radically altered the course of European history, and Henry V regained the crown of France through his determination, will to succeed and the sheer pugnacity of his 'happy few'; his 'band of brothers'.

The French should never have met the English and Welsh in open battle. From previous heavy defeats at Crécy (1346) and Poitiers (1356), they had reason to fear the longbow of the English and Welsh archers, who could each accurately fire a dozen or more armour-piercing bodkin arrows a minute. In the reloading stakes the French crossbows were no match. Legend has it the French feared the archers so much that they threatened to cut off the two fingers on the drawing hands of every one of them if they were captured.

At the end of the battle when the hundreds of Frenchmen were paraded through the ranks of archers (those who were fortunate enough to be spared because they were rich enough to attract a ransom), the archers showed them their two fingers – the V sign that has since become the British gesture of defiance.[1]

---

1 Who knows, and who cares whether or not this is a myth? It's still a great story and a fabulous metaphor.

The reasons why Henry V won against overwhelming odds?

1. The French had no effective leadership, but the English and Welsh had a strong and determined leader in King Henry V.

2. The English and Welsh were more flexible and manoeuvrable than the French, who came at them in a way that bunched them together and tripped them over so that many simply drowned in the mud.

3. The English and Welsh archers did not wear the heavy plate armour that encumbered the French men-of-war. The French got bogged down in the muddy field and once they were down in the mud, the archers moved in swiftly to dispatch them with their poleaxes and knives.

4. The awesome firepower of the English and Welsh longbows was a significant factor. It 'did for' the first and only French cavalry charge that was meant to destroy the archers.

5. The English and Welsh had very little left to lose and nowhere to go but forward.

Anyone with a modicum of insight will see that there are several parallels here with the battle between the institutional VLE and Edupunk 'do-it-yourself' personal Web tools. The shiny, expensive and cumbersome VLE dominates the battlefield that is education, and is supposedly the killer application that all colleges and universities have bought into.

The colour of the banner doesn't matter, because whatever the brand, the VLE has essentially a common architecture and purpose: it is there to restrict access, deliver homogenous content and control the activities of its users. It lumbers ever forward into confined spaces, tripping itself over as it goes, and is slow to adapt to new requirements. Whilst its champions think it is invincible, they don't seem to realise that it is becoming bogged down in a morass of apathy, resistance to use and lack of response to change.

By contrast, the personal Web moves along lightly at the pace of its users, being directed as changes and personal needs dictate. It has an awesome array of choices, and is responsive to the needs of communities of practice as well as the individual. It is cheap and not very attractive (at least in corporate terms) when compared to the institutional VLE, but it is a damned sight more effective when it comes to supporting learning. The institutional VLE is led by the entire institution and is therefore slow to respond to change, whilst the personal Web is determined by one user.

The personal Web has one more key advantage – it is owned by the individual who created it.

All things considered, it is inevitable that the personal Web will win in a straight fight against the institutional VLE. The VLE has had its day and will meet its demise, even though its supporters cannot see it coming. The personal Web is on the rise. For me and many, many others, we're showing our two fingers to the institutional VLE.[2]

Anatomy of a PLE

I worked alongside the University of Portsmouth's Manish Malik to reconceptualise PLEs, attempting to locate them across both informal and formal learning contexts. The research we did together raised more questions than it answered, but we were able to map out the finer details of our own notion of personal learning environments and tools. Our premise for the research was simple.

Firstly, if we were to understand personalised learning, we needed to know what a PLE looks like. We needed to examine its anatomy. What are its essential components? How does it differ from institutionally provided systems? Is there any common ground, and if so, how can this be harnessed? How can we offer students the best of both worlds – the security and protection of the institution and the freedom and creativity of the personal tool set?

These questions are yet to be addressed, but in our view the PLE extends beyond the Web tools students use to create, find, organise and share content. It is also wider than the personal learning network (PLN) of people and content that each of us generates

---

2 Steve Wheeler, 'Two Fingered Salute', Learning with 'e's (2009). Available online at: http://steve-wheeler.blogspot.com/2009/08/two-fingered-salute.html.

when we learn informally or in formal contexts. This is represented in the following figure:

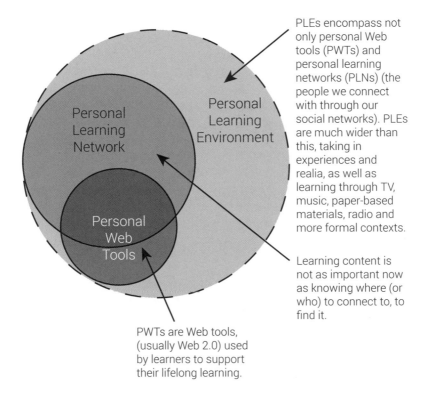

PLEs encompass not only personal Web tools (PWTs) and personal learning networks (PLNs) (the people we connect with through our social networks). PLEs are much wider than this, taking in experiences and realia, as well as learning through TV, music, paper-based materials, radio and more formal contexts.

Learning content is not as important now as knowing where (or who) to connect to, to find it.

PWTs are Web tools, (usually Web 2.0) used by learners to support their lifelong learning.

Anatomy of a personal learning environment

In the model below we propose a hybrid approach. Students require some structure and scaffolding when they first venture into digital learning environments, and a mixed ecology of institutional support and personalised media offers one possible solution. But first, let's deal with the key issues.

The biggest issue with the institutional Managed Learning Environment is that its design is dull, uninspiring and it is often difficult to navigate. Web 2.0 tools and services, known as the Cloud Learning Environment, are more attractive, easier to use and free, but are unprotected and vulnerable. Further, the content sent to the application ends up becoming the 'property' of the Internet company and is difficult to delete – a target for data mining. Whilst CLEs will not fully address all of the tensions between iMLEs and

PLEs, we argue that they provide a tentative bridge to provide the best of both worlds in terms of affordances and interoperability.[3]

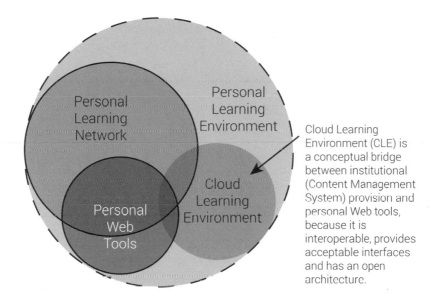

Cloud-based personal learning environment

Physiology of a PLE

As demonstrated in the diagrams, PLEs contain a variety of modes, layers and tools to support lifelong learning. Equally important as the components is the purpose of the personal learning environment. Each student will require different things from their PLE, but in essence these can be grouped into three main areas of activity.

The image below represents the three main functionalities I believe learners generally require to support lifelong learning in the digital age. You will note that the functionality is exclusive to the Personal Web Tools (PWTs) I outlined earlier. However, given that the context of the PLE is much wider than the Web tools a student uses, it is possible to apply creation, organisation and sharing of content

---

3   Steve Wheeler and Manish Malik, 'Personal Learning Environments: A Bridge in the Cloud?' Paper presented at the 1st PLE Conference, Barcelona, 2011.

to a wider range of practices, including analogue content such as newspapers and magazines, realia (visits, real experiences, encounters, conversations) and other non-digital materials. Whether these remain analogue or are in some way captured in digital format remains the choice of each individual lifelong learner.

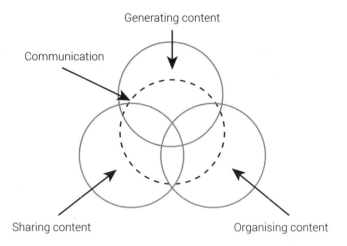

Functions of a personal learning environment

There are other functionalities, of course, but I believe that the essence of the physiology of most PLEs is represented in the diagram presented here. A fourth component of communication, which includes sharing, discussion and dialogue in both synchronous and asynchronous modes, can be represented as an overarching circle over the Venn diagram.

Personal Web Tools

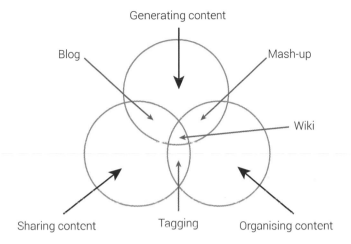

Physiology of a personal learning environment

Such key functions of the PLE – the personal Web tools component – can be managed through a number of tools, and learners will each have their individual preferences, all of which ensures that each PLE will be unique to that individual learner. Some of these tools are represented in the second figure, but these are by no means exhaustive, and of course, many are interchangeable for different tasks and purposes.

Note that in my model the e-portfolio sits across all functionalities and is the most likely tool to be provided by the institution or organisation, even though, by nature, it is also quite personal. Also of note is that wikis – collaborative online spaces where multiple users can create, edit and share content – are also tools that sit comfortably across all other functionalities. These concept maps provide a set of ideas which should offer a clearer view of how and why PLEs can be created, developed, managed and used by learners. For me, the concept of the personal learning environment connects closely to the idea I earlier discussed: cognitive technologies.

Digital storytelling

The power of technology can be harnessed to support our propensity to tell stories. The narrative seems to have been a part of human history since our cave dwelling days. We excel at it, it fuels our imagination, draws us together as a community, and makes us more knowledgeable about the world around us. We love to hear stories at any age, and broadcast media capitalise on this natural urge, presenting drama, documentaries and even news bulletins in narrative format. Storytelling has been a fundamental method for conveying knowledge since the dawn of education. With each new technology we are handed fresh opportunities to tell our stories in many new formats. We can create new forms of narrative and we can use our technologies as mind tools to amplify these stories to large audiences. In a post on digital storytelling, Aleks Krotoski[4] writes:

> Human experience is a series of never-ending, overlapping stories bumping into one another in expected and unexpected ways. Our days are made up of personal narratives of good and evil, joy and conflict, magic potions and angry gnomes.

I can happily subscribe to this. Every story has some representation of good and evil, dark and light or another opposing binary. As listeners and readers we can actively participate by translating other story elements to make the story our own. The magic potion in my part of the world would be cider, of course. Even the angry gnomes can be imagined here where I live in the south-west of England, although they are more likely to represent the frustrated tourists stuck in holiday traffic jams than mystical beings.

Stories can be incredibly powerful. Children like to listen to them, but they also like to write and tell their own, maybe what they did during their summer holidays – hopefully a long way from the traffic jams. Krotoski goes on to elaborate on why storytelling is so important, showing that our favourite narratives are created cooperatively, through a process that involves analysis and synthesis of familiar characters and events in our lives. Storytelling is our way

---

4   Aleks Krotoski, 'Storytelling: Digital Technology Allows us to Tell Tales in Innovative New Ways', *The Guardian*, 7 August, 2011. Available online at: http://www.theguardian.com/technology/2011/aug/07/digital-media-storytelling-internet.

of making sense of our worlds, and in essence storytellers become the curators of all kinds of diverse information which make up the structure of the narratives that explain our lives.

Storytelling is important to all of us, and not just because it is a legacy of our ancient cultures. Storytelling also goes beyond a mere collection of events. We tell the story of our lives when we meet someone new, and we relate the events of the day to our families and friends when we come home in the evenings. We make sense of the world around us, and order our priorities as we narrate our personal histories. We establish norms and decide what is important for our community. Krotoski asserts that one of the key functions of the narrative is as an aid to memory, or possibly that they point the direction to important aspects of living such as morality or spirituality. Whatever the format of the story, whether related as an oral presentation, a blockbuster movie, or even a bestselling novel, storytelling has the function of reinforcing societal norms, and tracing the history of who we are, our collective identity, the very essence of our humanity.

Storytelling is powerful because it is a route to making sense of our worlds – one of our prime motivators in life. It is our common search for the tacit knowledge that will enable us to survive and succeed. If something doesn't make sense, or if there is a clash of principles in our heads – a kind of cognitive dissonance – we make a concerted effort to try to resolve the conflict. That is how tacit learning happens. According to Thomas and Seely Brown,[5] you can't teach tacit knowledge. Unlike explicit knowledge, which is peddled every day in our schools in the form of lessons full of facts, this deeper tacit knowledge has to be experienced personally by each individual before it becomes theirs to own and to use. Storytelling takes each participant on a personal journey through a sometimes bewildering landscape of opportunities to acquire this kind of learning.

Digital storytelling can take our personal narratives up to a new plane of experience. The tools available to us today enable us to take companions on our journey through this terrain. We can co-create content, tell the story to each other regardless of location, and rework it so that it has common meaning and purpose. Our stories

---

5 Douglas Thomas and John Seely Brown, *A New Culture of Learning: Cultivating the Imagination for a World of Constant Change* (CreateSpace, 2011).

can be told time and time again, each time differently, with each version taking on a greater richness than its predecessor.

Is digital storytelling a radical departure from traditional education practices? I don't think so. We have been telling each other stories since the day we could string a sentence together. Children tell jokes in the playground. They write essays about what they did during their holidays. Children read Harry Potter and watch *EastEnders* on evening TV. It's something they are habituated to. Yet there is something new in the way our own stories can be generated, shared, repurposed and retold. The digital tools we now have at our disposal enable what Frank Rose[6] calls 'multi-way conversation'.

For Rose, storytelling has reached a new pitch, opening up space in a new social dimension. 'It's very different when you have a medium that forces you to engage with other people,' he says. 'You don't know if you're going to have to tell a story for one hour, two hours or ten years.'

Telling your story is an age-old cultural practice. Digital storytelling takes it to another level, involving global conversations, multiple versions, remixes and a cast of thousands. The radical aspect is realised when our understanding of the world around us can be transformed through these conversations. You don't need school for this kind of learning.

Living networks

My personal learning environment features many tools – creative, cognitive, connective – many of which act as technologies that extend and amplify my mind. These tools are embodied in and across a vast biological and technological network, a web made of individuals and their computers. They are the connected minds that act as my personal learning Web. These people are the nodes of the network and they are numerous. Many of them are known to me personally. Others are familiar to me from repeated online contact.

---

6   Frank Rose, *The Art of Immersion: How the Digital Generation is Remaking Hollywood, Madison Avenue and the Way We Tell Stories* (New York: W. W. Norton & Company, 2010).

Many more are less familiar, but each has a role to play and knowledge to exchange.

Personal Webs will assume increasing importance, not only for education, but for society in general. Such living networks, mediated through technology, are providing the new and invisible bonds that tie communities together. It is this 'digital cultural capital' that is beginning to define many of our professional activities. I edited a volume several years ago entitled *Connected Minds, Emerging Cultures* in which I featured a section on digital tribes. One quote from the chapter explains the notion of digital cultural capital:

> I will argue here that within the present information age, where digital communication technologies have fractured the tyranny of distance beyond repair, and where computers have become pervasive and ubiquitous, identification through digital mediation has become the new cultural capital. Cultural capital is the set of 'invisible bonds that tie a community together', without which societal cohesiveness begins to unravel. It is this 'social glue' – such mutual understandings and exchanges that occur on a daily basis – that holds together the basic building blocks of social life in which people simply look out for each other.[7]

This kind of scenario is played out every day, each hour on our social media and through other forms of digital mediation, as we connect with each other, share our experiences and stories, exchange artefacts, and care for our friends.

Extending just a little beyond my own personal learning Web, this living network and the tools at its disposal embrace all of the knowledge that humankind has ever accumulated, knowledge that is constantly being updated, revised, connected and expanded. Access for all to these vast resource repositories is provided through a bewildering array of device choices, offering a huge spectrum of possibilities.

The people, devices, connections and knowledge constitute the World Wide Web – a digital sea upon which float the products of the collective minds of this generation and those who have gone before.

---

7 Steve Wheeler, 'Digital Tribes, Virtual Clans', in S. Wheeler (ed.), *Connected Minds, Emerging Cultures* (Charlotte NC: Information Age, 2009): 65–76.

9

Measuring Learning in the Digital Age

When the cook tastes the soup, that's formative; when the guests taste the soup, that's summative.

Robert Stake

Assessment of learning will always be an important part of education. Teachers need to know how their students are progressing, and they rely on many different forms of assessment. It's also a legal requirement. Yet here again, we need to take care that education is advancing rather than stagnating. We need to ensure that assessment is not only accurate, but relevant and timely. As the world of work changes, so should teachers' conceptions of what it means to demonstrate new skills and knowledge, and how to measure that achievement appropriately.

Cathy Davidson[1] warns that in a world of work that is increasingly decentralised there are going to be new skills that we have no idea how to test. The stark fact is we know very little about what employers will be demanding from their workers in the next decade and beyond. We can speculate that employees will look for creative and innovative individuals, such as the Knowmads mentioned in an earlier chapter, but these skills are difficult to measure, and virtually impossible to teach.

How can we assess that which is difficult to measure and impossible to teach? All educators can do is create environments that are conducive for the propagation of these skills.

There are many different ways of measuring learning. Assessment is not solely about checking the standard of achievement; it's about

---

1 Cathy N. Davidson, *Now You See It: How Technology and Brain Science Will Transform Schools and Business for the 21st Century* (New York: Viking, 2011), p. 218.

enabling students to express their learning too. Good assessment also supports learning by providing learners with feedback on what they have done well and how they can improve in the future. It's important to get it right. Bad assessment may turn them off from learning for good. There is a growing consensus in the teaching profession that it is neither fair nor desirable to fail students. All students have a right to a grade, but no student should be told that they are a failure. Instead, perhaps we should agree that the word FAIL becomes an acronym: First Attempts In Learning. This is certainly how teachers should view assessment. It should not be used as a means to root out failures, but as a means to help all students to learn better and become the best they can possibly be in life.

There is also a dimension to assessment that transcends the teacher's role as an arbiter of knowledge, as a Demos report suggests:

> The best teachers constantly monitor what is happening to students as they set about learning and investigate when things do not proceed as planned or expected. They also inquire their own practice so they might get better at ensuring that their students learn successfully.[2]

Teachers can take the opportunity to use assessment as a way to improve their own learning. Using assessment processes as a means of testing their own performance moves the spotlight from the students and onto the pedagogy – exactly where it should be focused.

Fair measures

Overheard at a recent conference was a quote from a student who said 'Why can't we be tested on what we have learnt, instead of having to learn what we will be tested on?' Assessment drives what happens in schools, and is central to effective pedagogy, but how often do we get it right? Is the emphasis on testing what has been learnt, or on providing good feedback to support future learning?

The word assessment comes from the Latin *assidere*, which means 'to sit beside'. Today, assessment tends to be something students are

---

2 Demos, *About Learning. Report of the Learning Working Group* (London: Demos, 2004).

expected to deliver on their own. Assessment of learning is often an examination of what is inside the student's head.

Exams do little to help children learn deep and meaningful stuff they can later translate into the reality of life beyond the school gates. What exams teach children is that they can rote learn lots of facts, figures and information, and then manipulate the system. Educators then find themselves 'teaching to the test', just so that they can give their students a better chance at passing with a reasonable grade. However, being able to regurgitate this kind of surface knowledge onto a test paper to gain as high a grade as possible is as far removed from education as it is possible to be. Exams are at best a snapshot of students' memories at the time the test is administered. The exam itself tells us nothing about how children will cope with the messy, complex problems they will face in real life, or how good they are, for example, at working in a team. Exams tell us next to nothing about their creative abilities or their cognitive agility.

The knowledge and skills they have acquired need to be measured to see if they have actually learnt to the level expected by the examiner. Often, this is a stressful procedure, evoking anxiety and causing the student to become more focused on the content of their learning rather than its context. We know that many different kinds of assessment have been tried in schools. The current English secondary curriculum is based on a combination of summative (exams) and continuous (project-based) forms of assessment, and is thought to be fair because it measures learner performance and development over a longer period of time.

Yet it can be plausibly argued that this approach to assessment is flawed. It is flawed because it is based on a criterion referenced[3] system which expects all children within a given subject area (and usually within the same age group) to perform at a previously defined level of cognitive ability. It is a standardised testing system which is applied to a unique individual's learning – something that can never be 'standard'. On a positive note, it is fairer than an exam-only-based assessment where a pass or a fail may depend on the health or emotional state of the student at the time of the test.

---

3 Wikipedia, 'Criterion-Referenced Test'. Available online at: http://en.wikipedia. org/wiki/Criterion-referenced_assessment.

It is also fairer than norm referenced testing, which pits students against each other. But we could argue that criterion referenced assessment is still unfair for students whose cognitive skills are developing at a different rate to their peers, and who may not yet have the ability to perform at the expected criterion level. Many students subsequently fail and are stigmatised as a result of criterion referenced assessment. But it's the best we have, I hear some of you say. Well, if that's true, then we're all in deep trouble.

There are alternatives. One of the alternatives is a fairer and more personalised form of assessment which measures individual progress. It is known as ipsative assessment.[4] This is where learners are measured against their own previous performances. It is also a form of informal measurement of skill for children who compete against themselves in video games or in sports to gauge physical skills. Some would argue that there is no motivation better than competing against yourself – many professional sportsmen and women attest to this. If you fail, no one is able to pass judgement on you but yourself. If you succeed, that's the spur to push yourself onwards to gain even better skills or higher levels of knowledge. It does require a fair amount of self-regulation though. Ipsative forms of assessment have been successfully used for children with special educational needs.

How would ipsative assessment work in formal classroom settings? Well, there are already some hybrid versions of ipsative assessment being practised by some schools. For example, Assessing Pupil Progress (APP)[5] is a means of measuring learning over a period of time using the students' own previous attainment scores and mapping them against their current ones. APP is good for tracking progress of individuals over time and it also helps teachers to diagnose each pupil's learning issues and deficits early and to make intervention as required.

But this could be advanced to another level. What about letting students set their own criteria for assessment? How about some kind of negotiation with the teacher about what should be learnt and how it should be measured? Wouldn't this be more personalised? Some might view this as perhaps too radical, or possibly more time

---

4 Wikipedia, 'Ipsative Assessment'. Available online at: http://en.wikipedia.org/wiki/Ipsative.

5 Department for Education, *The National Strategies. National Archives.* Available online at: http://webarchive.nationalarchives.gov.uk/20131216163513/https://www.education.gov.uk/schools/toolsandinitiatives/nationalstrategies.

consuming, but it's also more tailored to the needs of each learner, and if it improves learning, wouldn't it be worth the extra effort?

Another method often overlooked by teachers, but one that is increasingly relevant in the digital age, is self-assessment. Younger students, for example, might be asked to report their learning on a spreadsheet or online space, using a graded self-appraisal form with category options such as: 'can do with help', 'can do on my own', and 'can show someone else'. Even if children are required to demonstrate their skill to a teacher, they can still complete the assessment form themselves, and thereby engender some personal pride and sense of achievement in their learning. If children design their assessment forms in conjunction with their teachers or peers, then additional learning is achieved, and they begin to understand the process of their own assessment more clearly. The form could also include a section where the child reports on what they have enjoyed and what they could have done better. The more a child is involved in their own assessment, the more valuable it will become to them.[6] Recent studies into the use of tablet computers to assess numeracy skills in Malawi and the United Kingdom has shown that children can triple their knowledge in mathematics in just eight weeks. The secret to this success is not only the self-driven nature and visual appeal of the content. The students are tested through the software on what they have learnt, and gain instant, relevant feedback on how well they have done.[7]

The following is a personal narrative of my experiences assessing undergraduate students:

Breaking the mould

A few years ago, I took the decision to encourage my university students to submit their assignments in forms other than the traditional, paper-based essay. It was a long overdue decision. For some time I had been agonising over whether we should persist in assessing students in modes of communication that they might

---

6 Peter John and Steve Wheeler, *The Digital Classroom* (London: Routledge, 2008).

7 PRWeb UK, 'Children in Malawi Triple Maths Knowledge in Just Eight Weeks Using EuroTalk Apps' (December 2013). Available online at: http://uk.prweb.com/releases/EuroTalk/Malawi/prweb11433155.htm.

never use in the real world. I therefore decided it was about time they were given some alternative opportunities to express their learning. Many of the modules I teach at my university deal with educational theory and practice. We often explore alternative methods of learning and teaching, and focus a great deal on new and emerging technologies. It was therefore both opportune and appropriate that I should lock assessment into the mode of learning and the subject matter.

That year most students played safe and kept to the familiar pathway by submitting standard essays, which was not a problem. However, a couple of students from the group were courageous enough to accept my challenge, and submitted their assignments in the form of blogs. Last year, several more students submitted their assignments in blog format, and one or two created videos as their assignments. Some told me it was a liberating experience and enabled them to express their learning more fully and honestly.

I believe this is a trend that will grow. Over the next few academic years I predict that submitting assignments in alternative digital formats will become the norm. They won't be 'alternative' any more, and institutions will need to adjust their practices to accommodate these new forms of assessment.

Here there are several questions to contemplate.

Firstly, teachers will need to know how to grade digital assignments, as they bear no resemblance to the traditional essay mode of assignment. To address this issue, teachers will need to agree with students on the assessment criteria and exactly what the marks will be awarded for. These assessment criteria should be equalised across all the possible submission formats. How, for example, might teachers agree an equivalency for an essay word count in a video? How should a blog be structured and sequenced when there may be several non-linear posts contained within it? Might a hyperlink in a blog be equivalent to a reference in an essay?

Other oblique issues will emerge due to the affordances the new media offer. For example, might students be graded on the quality of discussions on their blogs, and should likes, views, downloads and favourites on their video posting be taken into consideration? These questions are not exhaustive, but they are representative of the kind of thinking required to make sense of assessing non-traditional, digital-based assignments.

We need to support our learners as we work together through any new initiative. It may be prudent to present students with model assignments in blog, video, wiki and other non-traditional formats so they can see what they need to be aiming at. Modelling best practice is a very powerful approach and if applied appropriately through great exemplars, can offer cognitive apprenticeship to learners.

The second question is how can teachers ensure that students put the equivalent cognitive effort into a video as they would into a 4,000-word assignment? Can a 5-minute video contain the same level and quality of academic discussion as a 2,000-word essay? Or is it an easier option? Does a primary school student demonstrate what they have learnt with less or more effort in a photograph than they do in a painting? More importantly, will they learn more or less depending on the mode they choose?

Most crucially, teachers need to be aware of what is possible within the formats and technologies that students will use. For example, how difficult is it to put a voice-over track or a music track onto a video, or overlay captions? What are the synchronisation issues? How about problems with interoperability between differing formats? Has copyright been considered? If you don't know what the issues are, and the effort that is involved, you may be fooled into thinking students have worked hard (or not hard enough) to achieve the end product. Secondly, over a course of several months, it may be a good strategy to require students to create assignments in several formats, traditional and digital, so they gain an insight into what each can afford, and acquire skills in expressing their academic ideas and presenting their arguments in diverse ways.

Whatever you decide to do, it will be imperative that you ensure all assessment criteria are applied equally across all assignments, no matter what wrapper they are presented in. I'm quite clear with my students. Good structure, good grammar and readability (or watchability), critical analysis and evaluation, good data application and presentation, clear arguments and acknowledgement of sources – all of these must be evidenced in the assignment I give to my students, no matter what the format. It's up to them how they represent these components in their work.

There are further procedural and administrative issues that each institution will surely have to deal with. What if support services cannot (or will not) accommodate the submission of non-paper assignments? What if your external examiner is unwilling to accept blogs, wikis or videos as legitimate academic evidence of learning? For the first issue, it all depends on how your admin system is set up. Usually a few words or a friendly discussion with the relevant manager will be enough to adjust systems to enable admin staff to process non-linear and/or non-paper-based assignments.

As for the second issue – I would advise that you consider finding a new external examiner.

10
Global Educators

Multimedia brought the world into your classroom. Social media will take your classroom into the world.

Steve Wheeler

I want to inspire you to reach further. If you're a teacher, you almost certainly learnt and developed your skills in a classroom. Because of their training, most teachers have a mindset that is largely limited within four walls, the space where they and their students interact. Some may be fortunate enough to escape from the classroom to lead outdoor education trips, or work within a forest school, spending class time exploring and learning from their external surroundings. Some teachers are even fortunate enough to conduct a comparative studies trip or cultural visit to a foreign country.

Most teachers though, usually find themselves anchored within the four walls of the classroom or lecture hall for much of the academic year.

However, if we can access social media tools, each of us has opportunities to reach much further. We can become global educators. All we need is something important to teach, and some technology to teach it with. There are many options, but one of the most powerful global educator technologies is the blog.

Blogging as professional practice

There are many reasons why teachers should blog. The first is that blogging causes you to reflect. Donald Schon suggested that reflection on, in and through practice are vital components of any professional practice. Teachers naturally think back on what has happened in their classroom, and often wonder what they could have done better. Blogging can help with this process, enabling teachers to keep an ongoing personal record of their actions, decisions, thought processes, successes and failures, and issues they have had to deal with.

Another reason teachers should blog is that it can crystallise your thinking. In the act of writing, we invest a part of ourselves in the medium. The provisionality of the medium makes blogging conducive to drafting and redrafting. The act of composing and recomposing ideas can enable abstract thoughts to become more concrete. Your ideas are now on the screen in front of you; they can be stored, retrieved and reconstructed as your ideas become clearer. You don't have to publish your thoughts if you want to keep them to yourself. Save them and come back to them later. The blog can act as a kind of mirror to show you what you are thinking. Sometimes we don't really know what we are thinking until we actually write it down in a physical format.

Blogging can also give you personal momentum. Once you have started blogging, and you realise that you can actually do it, you will probably want to develop your skills further. Blogging can be time consuming, but the rewards make it worthwhile. In my own experience, I find myself breaking out of inertia to create some forward movement in my thinking, especially when I blog about 'edgy' topics that may be emotive, controversial or challenging. The more you blog, the better you become at writing for your audience, managing your arguments, defending your position and thinking critically.

Blogging can be creative. If you persist with blogging, you will discover that you develop new and creative ways to articulate what you want to say. As I write, I often search for alternative ways to express my thoughts. This can be diverse, through images, quotes, a retelling of old experiences through stories, videos, audio, or a useful hyperlink to related Web resources. You have many ways to convey your ideas, and you are only limited to your own imagination. Try out new ways of communicating and take risks. Blogging is a social media tool that encourages you to be creative.

Perhaps most importantly in the context of becoming a global educator, blogging can open up new audiences. You can become a teacher within an infinitely larger classroom, and as you blog on subjects you think are interesting, you will discover that there are plenty of other education professionals out there who are also interested. Such people will eventually find your blog and visit it regularly to see if they can learn something new from you.

It never ceases to amaze me how many students and colleagues contact me to tell me how much they have learnt from reading my blog. Some have told me how much it has inspired them to learn more, explore, take risks, and reach further. Others inform me that they have taken up blogging themselves. I greatly value such positive affirmation and I know this is also true with other edubloggers.

This is one of the main reasons I continue to invest my time in blogging. Knowing that what I'm writing and the rich subsequent dialogue are having a such positive impact on someone, somewhere in the world, is one of the main reasons I blog so regularly. I want to make a difference.

I once happened to stumble upon an interesting Twitter stream hashtag (#qaz11) – which I quickly realised was being generated by a group of students in the care of my old friend Jose Luis Garcia[1] who is at the University of Cantabria in Spain. Although the tweets were in Spanish, I was able to translate them using TweetDeck, and I followed for a while. The students were discussing the merits of the ten 'Teaching with Twitter'[2] activities I had posted on my blog. It was interesting to see them analyse and evaluate the potential of each activity within their own professional context as trainee teachers.

Without me actually being there, my thoughts were having an impact on the students' learning. It was gratifying to see that my ideas were helping them to frame their thinking, promoting discussion and encouraging them to engage critically with the topic.

The same is happening all over the world, every hour, every day, as teachers begin to share their ideas, advice, best practice and top tips across a global platform – the blog. We have become a new breed of teacher. Quite literally, we have become worldwide educators, with students in every country of the world reading our blogs, thinking, arguing, learning and then going off to try out some ideas.

---

1 Jose Luis Garcia, *Didactics: Higher Education and Teacher Training* [blog]. Available online at: http://nnttunican.blogspot.com/.

2 Steve Wheeler, 'Teaching with Twitter', Learning with 'e's (2009). Available online at: http://steve-wheeler.blogspot.com/2009/01/teaching-with-twitter.html.

We don't always see them, and we may never actually meet them, but they are there, and they are learning.

More tools for connected educators

My key message to all teachers in this chapter is: don't limit yourself to seeing the four walls of your classroom as the full extent of your world. Reach further – and become a worldwide educator. You have the technology.

Recently I have been considering the changing role of teachers who are adopting technology to extend the walls of their classrooms. These are a new breed of teachers who do not necessarily accept that the space for learning should be contained within four walls. In effect, through the use of social media and telecommunication technologies, these teachers are becoming global educators.

I consider myself a global educator and have articulated my ideas[3] on why this is a different approach to that of traditional teaching. Teachers who use technology to breach the classroom walls and share their content with others are connected educators, linked in to a number of powerful global communities of practice. As such, they have access to resources, dialogue and audiences they would not enjoy in a traditional learning and teaching role. But what tools do connected educators use to enable them to connect with these communities, resources, and audiences around the globe? Here are a few more tools I personally use:

Webinar

The first is the webinar, which is essentially a seminar run on the Web. Webinars are presented using software that enables the presentation of slides, videos, and communication through audio, visual and text channels. Some refer to this as a 'point-to-multipoint video conference', but webinars extend the video conference to other affordances.

---

3   Steve Wheeler, 'Connected Educators', Learning with 'e's (2011). Available online at: http://steve-wheeler.blogspot.com/2011/11/connected-educators.html.

There are a number of ways to teach and present live from beyond the classroom using webinars. I regularly present live (synchronous) Web seminars and other teaching sessions from my home office, from a hotel room, and from just about anywhere else I may be where there is access to the Internet. I have presented from Australia to the USA (there is a strange time zone difference between these two points) and from Europe to the USA, and in such events as the Reform Symposium, I have even presented to a worldwide audience of educators.

Webinar tools include Elluminate (now known as Blackboard Collaborate), WebEx and Adobe Connect, all of which have similar screen topographies and perform similar functions, but all have an associated cost. All of the above tools support live audio (you should use a headset to maintain quality), video communication (a webcam or internal camera on a laptop is needed for this), slideshow presentation tools and text communication. Webinars could also be conducted on Skype, which is currently free, but video and audio quality may be more variable using this tool.

Twitter

Twitter has provided me with some of the most powerful professional development I have ever had. I don't claim this lightly. Reflecting on almost thirty years of continuous professional development and in-service training I have to say that my personal network of contacts on Twitter provide me with the richest, most up to date and relevant content I have ever received. All I have to do is turn on my computer and follow the stream.

This social networking tool is deceptively simple but deeply sophisticated and versatile due to its inherent filtering facilities. It is also an excellent connecting tool – retweets are not repetition, they are amplification of content. The power of Twitter lies not only in its simplicity but also in its accessibility. It is a free public platform for communication.

Whether used as a backchannel to amplify an event, or as a closed channel to converse between small groups, Twitter enables a great deal more expression than one would expect from a 140 character limit. Hyperlinks and other media links can be shared, and the application of a URL shortener can create more space for a few annotations. Used in conjunction with the other tools showcased here, it is indeed a very powerful tool for the global educator.

Video

Social media tools such as YouTube and Vimeo are maturing into sophisticated tools that enable all kinds of visual media sharing. At the time of writing over 70 hours of video footage is uploaded to the YouTube servers every minute. Most of it can be disregarded as spurious, but some content found on YouTube is pure gold dust for teachers.

It is now possible to create your own personal channel on the service simply by clicking a few buttons. There is an editing facility available that allows teachers to select specific sequences of video and create new versions to show students. Embed codes and other sharing options allow teachers to disseminate their videos to a wide audience through blogging, on wikis and via social media.

The comments box at the foot of each video clip enables dialogue between presenter and students. It's asynchronous, but has the capability to be a highly effective method of sending quality content to distributed learners.

Slide sharing

If you have a PowerPoint slideshow presentation or a document you want to share with a wider audience then SlideShare should probably be your first social media choice. Several of my recent presentations have gone viral simply because the tool is easy to access and is being used by large numbers of people every day. You can see at a glance how many views your slideshow has received, as well as how many favourites, downloads and embeds; and most importantly, you can respond to comments to develop interesting dialogue with your remote visitors and students.

These are just a few of the vast array of tools that are currently available to the global educator, and they are my preferences. None of this matters if you want to keep your content to yourself and protect it with copyright, but sharing your content for free opens up a whole new vista of possibilities.

This is where open scholarship comes into play.

Open scholarship

Most of us by now are familiar with open learning, and many could describe their use of open source software such as Moodle, Mahara, Linux or OpenOffice. Many can also articulate what open educational resources look like, and have knowledge of Massive Open Online Courses (MOOCs) and other open methods of education. The concept of open scholarship will have a significant impact on the future of education.

There is a complex interplay between openness, scholarship and digital technology. Some writers such as Robin Goodfellow[4] argue that it is an impossible triangle to reconcile. Others, including the Council for Australian University Librarians, are more optimistic, suggesting that open scholarship is achievable, not least in the aim of open collaboration and development to promote openness in all aspects of education.

For me, open scholarship is a state of mind – it is a choice each educator needs to make as to how open they wish to be, along an entire spectrum of scholarly activities. Some educators are closed in the sharing of their content but are open to collaboration with other educators. But true openness is where content is shared freely, all work is attributed fairly, and where educators also open themselves up for dialogue, collaboration and constructive criticism.

Truly open scholars are those who have aspirations to be global educators, promoting free learning for all, reaching out and connecting with other educators and learners everywhere, with the aim of participating fully in their worldwide community of practice.

---

4 Robin Goodfellow, 'Scholarly, Digital, Open: an Impossible Triangle?' *Research in Learning Technology* 21 (2014). Available online at: http://dx.doi. org/10.3402/rlt.v21.21366.

Openness in education

It seems perverse that in the 21st century, in a time of economic crisis, where the world desperately needs education, that we hoard it and preserve it solely for the elite. If we believe education is a fundamental human right, then we will do what it takes to provide good, affordable, accessible opportunities for people to learn the important things they will need to survive in a hostile, uncertain world. And yet, 500 million children remain outside of education because they cannot afford to attend. The problem we face in the 21st century is how to educate everyone.

We have enough money to make it happen. But the old problem is never resolved.

In a keynote speech I gave at the Solstice Conference in June 2012 at Edge Hill University, I argued that we need to be more open about our content and tools, ownership of learning, intellectual property and even the very practices we participate in on a daily basis – open scholarship. I spoke about Creative Commons, open source software, open access journals, open educational resources, community-led initiatives such as MOOCs, and the whole idea about being open and sharing learning. These ideas may not fully address the problem of how to educate everyone, but at least we will make a start by making learning more accessible.

Knowledge is like love. You can give it away as much as you like, but you never lose it. The more we give away our knowledge, the more we are educating our world, and the more we are fulfilling our destinies as global educators.

Never before have there been so many opportunities to make contact with educators worldwide, many of whom have wonderful creative ideas to exchange. Indeed, the fact that so many social media users are altruistic and are willing to share their ideas with their community for free should be enough to convince most educators to join in.

Clay Shirky was insightful when he wrote the following:

> The use of social technology is much less determined by the tool itself; when we use a network, the most important asset we get is access to one another.

> We want to be connected to one another, a desire that … our use of social media actually engages.[5]

The last line gives it away.

As humans, we have an innate need to talk to others, to share and compare, reify our own ideas, learn from each other, and gain a sense of belonging in a group of like-minded others. This is a deep-seated human trait that many psychologists have researched down through the years. Fundamental to Abraham Maslow's hierarchy of human needs[6] is the notion of 'belonging' to a group and gaining respect from others.

Share and share alike

There are many benefits to openness, to which many teachers who share their content will attest. My own experience of freely sharing my content has opened up countless new opportunities for me as a global educator.

I will never forget the first time one of my articles was translated into another language. It was only the abstract, but it was translated into three languages – Spanish, French and German – for inclusion in an edition of the international peer-reviewed journal *Educational Media International*. I don't know who they found to do it, or how long it took. Just the fact that I was published, and in four different languages, was impressive to me. EMI probably had to pay several people to translate my article, along with all the other articles that appear in the journal, but now all that is changing.

Since I took the decision to offer all my blog posts, slideshows and other content for free under a Creative Commons Licence, allowing anyone to freely copy and also repurpose my work, some interesting things have happened. Firstly, I haven't lost any of my work. It still belongs to me, and anyone who decides to use it attributes it to me. Secondly, my work is being amplified. It is spreading farther afield

---

5 Clay Shirky, *Cognitive Surplus: Creativity and Generosity in a Connected Age* (London: Penguin, 2010), p. 14.

6 Abraham H. Maslow, *Motivation and Personality* (New York: Harper, 1954).

than I could ever have hoped it would. It is being cited in other people's work, and it is also being translated into other languages.

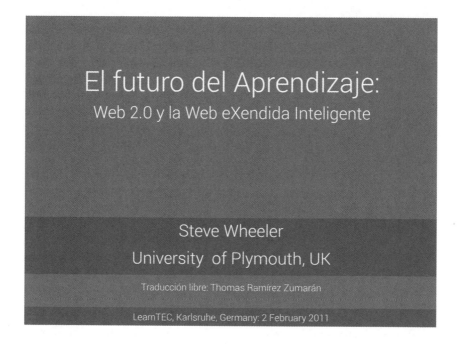

The slideshow above, along with several others, has been translated into Spanish, and now just about the entire Latin American world is aware of, and has access to, my work. It is remarkable that I didn't spend a single penny to get it translated, nor did I need to ask anyone to do it. People within the professional community of practice simply take it upon themselves to translate because they have a passion for sharing good content they have found in their peer network. The slideshow above was translated by Thomas Ramírez Zumarán, and in the first few days of publication it attracted around 8,000 views in addition to my original slideshow on SlideShare (which at the time of writing had reached almost 75,000 views).

Now people are taking on the task of translating my blog posts too. Some of my content was recently translated into French by Frédéric Domon. Here's the opening paragraph of one of my blog posts called 'Is all learning social?'

Presque tous les jours, je me laisse entraîner dans des discussions autour des fondamentaux de l'apprentissage, de la nature de la connaissance et des processus d'éducation. Cela va de pair avec le métier de professeur à l'Université et je m'attends à me retrouver dans cette situation très souvent. Lorsque je ne parle pas d'apprentissage, j'y réfléchis, je lis, fais des recherches ou écris à ce sujet.

Again, I didn't need to ask for this to be done, and neither did the translator need to ask my permission. Permission to repurpose the post was self-evident in the Creative Commons Licence I attach to the foot of every blog post. My blogs and slideshows are now appearing in other languages without any effort on my part. I'm very happy that they are, because now language is no longer a barrier to understanding. My ideas are out there for all to read, share and discuss, and that is reward enough for offering my work for free.

Considering the above, I'm convinced that education needs to be open and globalised. As we develop personal expertise and begin to practise it in applied contexts, so we need to connect with global communities. This is, in effect, the sharing of one's practice across a peer network to obtain informal scrutiny, appraisal and feedback. This has many useful functions. Students who share their content online can obtain a worldwide audience who are willing to act as a peer network to provide constructive feedback.

Teachers can crowd-source their ideas and share their content in professional forums and global learning collectives, or harness the power of social media to access thought leaders in their particular field of expertise. And teachers can be open scholars, connected to and receptive of the support of their global professional community.

It goes without saying that those scholars who are not connected to the global community are increasingly isolated and will in time be left behind as education advances.

11
Learning on the Move

Mobile phones are misnamed. They should be called gateways to human knowledge.

Ray Kurzweil

There are now more mobile phones in the world than there are people. At the time of writing, mobile phone subscriptions have passed the eight billion mark, and there is no sign that this trend is slowing. Mobile phones have transformed the lives and relationships of many millions worldwide, some for better, some for worse. The small, smart device you carry with you everywhere has raw computing power that can connect you to the Web; capture and store images, audio and video; and tell you exactly where you are on the planet.

Smartphones are increasingly pervasive and accessible and continue to disrupt many aspects of our society. They are influencing our decisions about how we interact with each other, access and consume information, work, entertain ourselves and purchase our goods. Will smartphones also transform education?

Always on

Mobile devices provide wonderful new opportunities for learning. Students no longer need to be location dependent. Mobiles facilitate personalised learning while they are on the move, and enable them to access the Web wherever they are. These two factors alone would be enough to tip the balance and convince most people that some kind of step change is taking place, but mobile learning can take us so much further.

Dan Pontefract, Chief Envisioner at TELUS, believes mobile technology will impact on education by supporting 'pervasive learning – learning at the speed of need through formal, informal, and social modalities'.[1] He is right, and a priority for future educators should be to ensure that students have access to just in time and just enough learning. Consider the idea that learners are 'always on'. This is sometimes used as a derogatory description of younger users of mobile devices. From a negative perspective the 'always on' generation is seen as shallow, easily distracted and lacking in any critical reasoning abilities. This may be true for some, but it's an unfair generalisation. That fact is that learners today are doing things differently, whether they are in schools, colleges or businesses. Users of mobile devices are breaking the mould of traditional learning formats, bypassing and shortcutting conventional modes of learning, and maximising the affordances of their personal devices to support their learning in impressive ways.

In my own professional experience, younger students are usually thoughtful, critically aware and reasoned when learning with technology. Granted, we have all witnessed some frivolous uses of mobile devices, but putting these to one side, let's consider the benefits. Students can use their personal technology to interact with content at a much deeper level than we were able to do in the days before we had such tools. Learning in their own time and at their own pace while on the move gives them more time to reflect on their learning. They can easily connect with other students informally, and can support each other outside of the school or university context. Furthermore, their learning can be built upon at any time, and in any place, because students take all their content with them wherever they go.

'Always on' should therefore also be seen as a positive phenomenon. They just need good pedagogy to stay focused.

Here is a quote taken from '12 Principles of Mobile Learning' by Terry Heick:

> Always-on learning is self-actuated, spontaneous, iterative, and recursive. There is a persistent need for information access, cognitive reflection, and interdependent function through mobile devices. It is also embedded in communities capable of intimate and natural interaction with students.[2]

---

1   Dan Pontefract, *Flat Army: Creating a Connected and Engaged Organization* (Hoboken NJ: Jossey-Bass, 2013).
2   Terry Heick, '12 Principles of Mobile Learning', TeachThought Blog (2012). Available online at: http://www.teachthought.com/technology/12-principles-of-mobile-learning/.

School leaders who refuse to support this kind of learning are myopic. They also put their schools in danger of being left behind as others move ahead. All the contrived arguments that are thrown against the integration of personal digital devices in the classroom fall by the wayside when educators commit to promote self-driven learning. It is difficult to argue against the trend of personalised, mobile devices and its positive impact on learning.

The 'always on' trend, in particular, offers huge potential in the workplace and in traditional education spaces. If mobile devices can be freely harnessed, we can expect to see exciting new developments in education and the emergence of new forms of learning. One interesting new form of learning is called digital curation.

Mobile digital curation

What is digital curation? For those who visit museums or galleries, curators are experts in a specific genre of exhibit, and ensure that the displays are kept up to date, accurate and relevant for the viewing public. Curation is at the very heart of the success of any museum or art gallery and digital curation is similar in many ways. It is becoming more important as content increases.

Mitch Kapor once declared that getting information off the Internet is like taking a drink from a fire hydrant. It does feel like that sometimes. We are regularly exposed to a tsunami of content, and we are in danger of being swamped by it every minute we are online. Finding what you want is not usually a problem – Google and other advanced search engines ensure that. Organising and managing it is much more difficult.

Curation of content is one specific response to the problem of information overload. Curation takes content management one step further than aggregation of content – it involves organising and adding value to that content once it is aggregated. There are many tools and services now available to users to help them curate content. Some are fairly easy to use, enabling users to share content they find in an organised and highly visual manner. Scoop.it and Pearltrees are useful for this purpose. Others allow you to create a sequence of content, perhaps stuff that you have gathered from a conference or other event. Storify is very useful if you want to do this kind of curation.

Perhaps the most useful and versatile curation tool is Diigo, which enables you to do all of the above, and also take snapshots of websites so you can revisit them, even if they suddenly disappear.

Mobile learners can capitalise extensively on the many features of curation tools as they are ideally suited for the task of curation on the move. They can adapt to the style and personal preferences of users to store content, publish ideas and connect learners. Smartphones ensure that curation takes on a continuous process that transcends the user's ability. There is one more aspect – mobile content curation also enables users to interact with their environments more meaningfully (for example, augmented and mixed reality, as well as GPS services).

There is a design issue. It's important for teachers and learners that tools are transparent – they should be so simple to use that the user thinks more about learning than they do about how they will operate the tool. It's a complete waste of time if a student spends more time trying to figure out how to navigate a website than they do focusing on its content. In a recent Web interview I was asked what impact I thought mobile devices will have on learning. I replied that the proliferation of mobile devices is only going to drive user-generated content in one direction: upwards.

Content will always increase rather than decrease. If we all became mobile curators, content could be organised in such a way that learning would be enhanced, extended, enriched and engaging rather than detached, confused and diffused.

Mobile learning and higher education

What of higher education? How can we expect to see mobile technologies influencing our university education systems? As the shift from location-specific learning to untethered learning continues to gather pace, personal devices such as smartphones and tablet computers will assume increasing importance, becoming an indispensable part of every student's toolkit. Distributed forms of learning such as MOOCs are burgeoning, and geographical distance between learners and their parent institutions is less of a problem. As has already been highlighted, this is partly because learners are intimately familiar with the capabilities of their own devices, and are able to use them to learn in creative and productive ways. They don't need to think too hard about how to get their devices to work – they simply use them as tools for learning. 'Bring Your Own Device' is now commonplace in universities, which means that students no longer need to study in a single location. If students are no longer required to be in the same place as their teachers, several things become apparent.

The first is that traditional spaces such as the lecture hall, computer suite and classroom assume less significance. Some would argue that the millions invested in building traditional rooms for education in the last few years might easily have been spent on more relevant and future-oriented projects. However, if physical spaces retain their importance for many universities, then the manner in which they are configured needs to be radically reviewed. Why, for example, are lecture halls still designed with fixed chairs in rows and tiers, thus limiting student interaction? Where do students plug their laptops, tablets and mobile phones when they need to recharge their batteries? Are today's lecture halls designed with enough power sockets within easy reach? Why do we still tether computers to desks, row upon row in computer suites? Does this not simply replicate the style of traditional lecture halls? Does computing still need to take place in a specific location? Generally, traditional education environments fail to support new approaches to learning. These are design issues that could be dealt with effectively at the planning stage, as patently such expensive resources could be deployed much more effectively.

Secondly, as I alluded to earlier in this section, the current pedagogy that underpins higher education is just as much in need of reform as it is in schools. Although the traditional lecture still has its place, it is looking increasingly out of place in an age where students are used to learning on the move. Delivery of content from a lectern is also strange and anachronistic in a time where much knowledge is shifting from objective certainty to subjective provisionality. A number of effective alternatives are possible when each student owns a mobile personal learning device to accommodate their individual needs. Learning becomes more self-directed, and students get involved in creating knowledge as well as receiving it. They also become more active and wide-ranging in their learning approach.

Universities should be a place where students actively seek out and create new and previously undiscovered knowledge, rather than passively consuming knowledge that already exists.

Collaborative learning activities become more feasible, and can extend beyond traditional times and physical locations. Learning through making, doing and problem solving is extended as students are no longer constrained by class times and physical boundaries. Ultimately, the role of the educator changes, as lecturers assume a supportive and facilitative role rather than a directive one. Lecturers and professors retain their roles as experts, but acknowledge that their students can also bring knowledge to the learning process, and can also teach each other.

Thirdly, if students are now connecting remotely to campus services, the development of digital content and the provision of better communication channels is essential to ensure the success of distributed and distance learning methods. If students study exclusively or predominantly away from the traditional campus, their prime connection to peers, experts and content will be through their personal devices. If the infrastructure to support this fails for any reason, students are suddenly separated from their resources and expert support. Universities must therefore ensure that institutional services such as Learning Management Systems and the provision of other centralised software remain stable and accessible at all times.

As the personal device becomes more prevalent among student populations, so universities will need to reappraise their strategies for course provision. One of the most important decisions to be made is how to ensure that student expectations are met, whether they attend the traditional campus or not. An important issue that is often raised when students study away from their traditional learning spaces is how to ensure that interaction and dialogue are possible anywhere and at any time. Whilst this is not always possible, it is, nevertheless, something that the leading higher education institutions are trying hard to address. For everyone involved in this process, a sound understanding of the theoretical basis of interaction is highly recommended.

Mobile technology and blended interaction

Veteran education theorist Michael G. Moore once wrote about three types of interaction.[3]

The first, learner–teacher, is the most likely kind of interaction to be found in traditional classroom settings, but with the age of social media and other forms of digitally mediated communication interaction can now be just as rich an experience when conducted at a distance.

The second type of interaction is the learner–learner kind. Generally, this kind of interaction can be seen in the informal conversations that take place outside the classroom, in the common room or waiting for the bus home. And yet, in formal learning settings, learner–learner interaction can be used as a valuable pedagogical technique to encourage free thinking, deeper engagement with the topic, debate and discursive activities, collaborative learning and much more. Increasingly we are also witnessing students interacting with their peers through Facebook pages and other social media sites they have set up themselves.

Moore's third kind of interaction is learner–content. This is probably the least formal of the interactions in terms of its place in the classroom. Although some learner–content interaction can be observed in the classroom, with the momentum now toward more discussion, project work and collaborative learning within the classroom, student–content interaction is more likely to occur outside the classroom – at home, at work, on journeys. The flipped classroom concept takes advantage of technology to promote student–content interaction outside of the classroom.

---

3 Michael G. Moore, 'Editorial: Three types of interaction', *The American Journal of Distance Education*, 3, 2: (1989).

Interactions of the fourth kind

Other theorists have subsequently expanded on this interactional triumvirate. In 1994, Hillman, Willis and Gunawardena[4] suggested a fourth kind of interaction which they called student–interface. This is the interaction students have with the devices they are using to support their learning. Their proposal reflected not only the proliferation of computer technologies but also a growing interest in Human Computer Interaction (HCI) and cognitive science. In the digital age, this is the first point of contact between students and all other kinds of interaction.

Students now interact more or less continually with their peers and with their tutors. The article called for 'design strategies that facilitate students' acquisition of the skills needed to participate effectively in the electronic classroom'. Hillman et al. hit the nail on the head two decades ago, just as new computer systems were beginning to emerge. Now, more than ever, effort should be put into understanding how learners interact with their tools and technologies.

How, for example, might students learn differently using touch surfaces such as the iPad, when compared to non-touch devices such as the Xbox 360 Kinect? There is discussion about the advantages of game playing using haptic perception (the sense of resistance and tactile feedback) devices such as the Nintendo Wii handset over powerful gestural but non-touch controlled interfaces. What about the several human senses that are brought into play when such tools are used? What can we learn about ourselves and our environments when proprioception (the relative position of our limbs and body in relation to each other) and equilibrioception (the sense of body movement, balance and acceleration) are called into use? For a long time we have focused on the main senses (audio and visual, and to a lesser extent kinaesthetic) at the expense of other senses, but with new technologies increasingly available for learning, it is now time to study the effects of the fourth kind of interaction in greater detail.

---

4 Daniel Hillman, Deborah Willis and Charlotte Gunawardena, 'Learner Interface Interaction in Distance Education', *The American Journal of Distance Education* 8.2 (1994).

The advent of mobile communication has expanded this taxonomy still further. The use of mobile phones is liberating learners to interact in many new ways and in many different contexts. Consider the benefits of learning while on the move. Once this could only be achieved using books, and of course this is still a widespread and relevant activity for learning. I want to argue here, though, that personal, handheld technologies such as smartphones, e-readers, tablet computers and games consoles enable *interactive* mobile learning conducted at the pace of the individual, in any place and at any time.

Let's assume for the moment that we can connect to the Web from anywhere we are, and that everyone has a mobile device. Although this is far from reality, we might concede that if such a thing were possible, it would represent a paradigm shift for education and a personalised learning revolution for every student.

Learners would not only be able to learn whilst traversing any environment, they would experience continuous, seamless delivery of content, interaction with their tutors and connections with their fellow students, or interpersonal interaction. They would also be able to interact with their environment and objects within it, known as extrapersonal interaction, and also with objects within their personal space such as the interface of their device, referred to as peripersonal interaction.

The power of thought

Intrapersonal interaction is inevitable, including the process of internal dialogue with self, thoughts and reflections.

This happens in all learning contexts, because it is the internal talk learners have with themselves as they assimilate knowledge, and reason, analyse, evaluate and reflect on their experiences. The difference here though is that mobile learners will be in a place of their own choosing, and will continue the internal self-talk whilst in total and perpetual contact with others and with their content.

We can speculate that this internal interaction has the potential to be amplified through the mobile device to the network of peers, propagated across multiple interactions. What I am arguing for here is that the power of thinking (intrapersonal) can be amplified across the network, provoking dialogue (interpersonal), while each member of that network interacts with their devices (peripersonal) and environments (extrapersonal). What's more, I believe when using mobile devices, it is possible that these multiple interactions can be both blended and simultaneous.

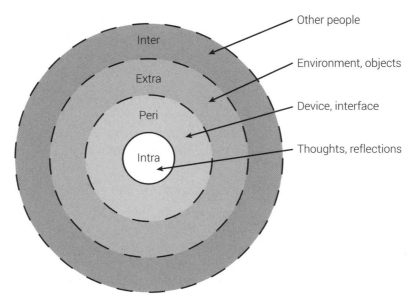

Modes of interaction

I should also add that the advent of the smartphone brings with it the ability to transcend many of the previously insurmountable barriers to good interpersonal communication, including language, culture and distance. There's a mobile app for everything, or if not, there soon will be. We are only just beginning to appreciate and comprehend the disruptive and transformational potential the mobile phone brings to learning.

Mobile gives the edge

As has been highlighted in previous chapters, every innovation brings a certain amount of disruption. Most significantly for those who are immersed in schools, colleges and universities, mobile technology is disrupting education. There are many examples of the positive disruptive effects of mobile phones on education. How can such a small object be so disruptive?

Firstly, mobile technology is disruptive because it creates location-independent learning opportunities. When students are no longer tethered to specific locations such as classrooms or computer suites, new and different types of learning become possible, and in many cases, inevitable. Students who are on the move can interact directly with their environments in more meaningful ways when they have mobile phones. They can engage with learning content with more freedom. They are no longer location dependent but they are still connected, and can maximise their available time to learn whenever they want and wherever they find themselves.

Potentially, there is no more 'down time' when students have a mobile device in their hands. It's a jaded expression now, but 'anytime, anyplace' learning is not only within the reach of most of us, for many it is already commonplace. Furthermore, the available infrastructure is becoming less of an issue.

Arguably, students are no longer completely reliant on Internet connectivity with the advent of the mobile app and the capability to download vast amounts of data during the times they do have a Wi-Fi connection.

Secondly, mobile technology is disruptive because it encourages students to be more creative. Students now have the capability to capture images and audio and video recordings of their experiences wherever they are. The creation, repurposing and sharing of content has never been easier.

Potentially, with new augmented reality and wearable technologies emerging, we will be able to 'lifelog'; that is, we will be able to make a record of every minute of our lives if we so wish. One of my students remarked in a recent lesson that her 'entire life' was stored in a small device. The danger here, of course, is the calamitous potential of losing your mobile phone or having it stolen.

Thirdly, mobile technology can be richly social. Access to powerful social media sites enables students to maintain perpetual contact with their peers, family and tutors, providing constant new opportunities to learn informally, on the move, and in many modes and formats. Howard Rheingold[5] argued as early as 2002 that mobile phones harness the 'power of the many', which has manifested itself in recent years in social phenomena such as citizen journalism, flash mobs and crowd-sourced funding projects.

We need to be aware though that clashes between authority and individual use of disruptive technology is problematic, and as Jon Agar[6] pointed out, there are fierce tensions between centralised power and the democracy afforded by mobile technology. Other warnings about the social and cultural challenges of mobile technology disruption, and the capability of mobile tools to distract, have been articulated by Mark Curtis in his book *Distraction: Being Human in the Digital Age.*[7]

Finally, mobile technology is disruptive because it enables personalised learning within social contexts. Each student is uniquely individual, and each can create their own 'desire lines' and personalised pathways to learning through the flexibility of smart devices and tools. Smartphones are crammed full of useful technologies that can support creative learning. We are witnessing only the beginnings of the radical disruption of education that will be possible with mobile technology. We can only speculate on what will happen when the convergence of GPS, cameras, augmented reality, voice control and mobility becomes mainstream, and everyone has access to information about everything, everywhere.

What happens when all objects you encounter are context aware, and your mobile phone helps you to interact with them and learn from them? Whatever happens will be totally different from anything we can currently do in education. Smartphones will certainly give learning the edge, and will help teachers to become digitally ready and digitally fluent.

---

5   Howard Rheingold, *Smart Mobs: The Next Social Revolution* (New York: Basic Books, 2007).

6   Jon Agar, *Constant touch: A Global History of the Mobile Phone* (Cambridge: Icon Books, 2013).

7   Mark Curtis, *Distraction: Being Human in the Digital Age* (London: Futuretext, 2004).

12 Literacy in a Connected World

Education is simply the soul of a society as it passes from one generation to another.

Gilbert K. Chesterton

When we were in school we learnt how to read and write, skills that eventually became known as literacy. Later on, schools developed other elements for the literacy curriculum, including speaking and listening. Obviously, all of these skills are vital to prepare children for a world of work.

With the digital age now upon us, these skills have been adapted and have evolved and expanded into a range of skills that translate to the use of technology. In a time when all students need to be 'digitally ready', the 3 'R's (reading, writing and arithmetic) are gradually being supplemented by other literacies. You won't find these new literacies in most school curricula, nor will you often see them formally taught. Instead, students typically learn the new literacies through a process of cultural transmission as they immerse themselves in social media and smartphone communication.

It would also be fair to say that many of the new, so-called digital literacies are still emerging, and are more or less being made up as we go along. Because we communicate in so many different modes, using so many diverse tools and technologies, there is some confusion over what is required and what is acceptable. This has led media and literacy experts such as Gunther Kress[1] to call for a new way of thinking about literacy. Kress argues that making meaning in writing and making meaning in reading both need to be rethought in an age where multimodality is commonplace.

Many of the new literacies expressed in popular culture are a result of the use of technology. Lankshear and Knobel identify several, including digital remixes, content mash-ups and image

---

1 Gunther Kress, *Literacy in the New Media Age* (London: Routledge, 2009).

Photoshopping; all essentially reworkings of what already exists.[2] Many of these transgress the boundaries of what we once considered to be literacy. How do students and teachers in the digital age extract meaning from the bewildering array of content that is now available? The answer is that we all need to be digitally literate. We need to be digitally ready.

Digitally ready?

What does it mean to be digitally ready? How can we ascertain what is necessary for someone to be digitally literate? The answer may be changing just about every other month, as new devices, tools and services appear and are rapidly assimilated into the repertoire of individuals everywhere. Being skilled in operating computers and mobile phones may no longer be sufficient. Skill is a dexterity or ability that comes from your knowledge and aptitude and manifests itself in being able to do something well. Writing is a skill, but it is also a literacy – in fact it constitutes a set of literacies. Literacy extends beyond skill. Lankshear and Knobel[3] argued for the 'embeddedness' of literacy within wider social practices. Their reasoning was that the act of writing involves more than the reproduction of a sequence of letters, words, sentences and paragraphs. Words in isolation mean very little – it is their context that gives them meaning.

The literates of this century will be those who are intimately familiar with digital media, understand the culture, and can fully harness their tools to do their bidding. Those who are not digitally literate may find themselves on the periphery of the connected society. They will become a part of what is now known as the digital divide.

---

2 Colin Lankshear and Michele Knobel, *New Literacies: Everyday Practice and Classroom Learning* (New York: McGraw Hill, 2006).

3 Ibid.

Culture and consequence

We know that there are digital divides between those who have and those who don't have access to technology. Some divides are socio-economic; others are technical, based on geographical location and access to sufficient infrastructure; still others are about willingness to engage, or the ability to be able to use tools effectively.

Later in this chapter I will feature some of the digital literacies I consider to be vital for individuals who wish to effectively harness the potential of digital media and technology. In this chapter I will also map some of the skills for Learning 2.0, based on the work of Mark Federman.[4]

Skills and literacies are words that are often used interchangeably, and ostensibly this is not an issue. However, I think a clear distinction should be made if we wish to fully apprehend the many nuances and subtleties of learning with digital media. We are digitally ready when we are able to utilise our technologies effectively, and we are digitally literate when we are able to act appropriately and make reasonable decisions in the face of the relatively unfamiliar culture of the digital ecosystem. In the following section, I will offer some examples of literacies that derive from immersion in a culture.

During my formative years I spent two years living in Holland, where I attended an international school. Although most of our lessons were in English, some were in German, and I also picked up a fair understanding of Dutch. My family and I were visitors, and had to learn the subtle nuances and some of the intricacies of these languages to fully participate within our host culture. Basic conversational language was usually enough, but to appreciate the finer aspects of life in Holland and Germany, we also had to learn some of the idioms and some of the slang. However, spoken language is only a small part of culture. What we do is just as important as what we say.

I discovered that when visiting Islamic countries, or meeting Muslims, it is not acceptable for a man to touch a woman. Several

---

4 Mark Federman, 'Organization Effectiveness and Leadership Development: What is the (Next) Message' (2010). Available online at: http://whatisthemessage.blogspot.co.uk/2010_08_01_archive.html.

times I have seen colleagues embarrass themselves when they have tried to shake a Muslim woman's hand. In some Asian cultures it is offensive to show someone the bare sole of your foot. In other cultures, nudity is perfectly acceptable. In New Zealand it's very bad form for you to sit on a table. Culture consists of shared symbolism and understanding, passed down through interaction and observation. There is always a meaning behind the action, so when the symbolism isn't agreed or shared by everyone, problems arise. It's usually quite difficult for visitors to learn and understand these conventions.

While working on a project, I did a lot of driving around Midwest America, and found that I had to adjust and adapt my previously learnt driving skills to 'driving in another culture'. 30 years on from passing my driving test I consider myself fairly adept and practised at driving in the UK; in fact my driving skills have become competencies, and are usually unconscious and effortless. In the USA though, my skills were not sufficient. On the highways of America I needed to adapt to an alien environment of driving on the right side of the road and the left side of the car.

It took quite a lot of practice before I began to feel confident. The gear shift had to be done with my right hand, and there was a need for me to understand not only the unfamiliar road signs but also different conventions and the unwritten rules of driving in America. These were literacies that I had to build on around the basic skills I had already mastered while driving in the UK. I still made mistakes, some quite embarrassing, but the longer I drove around in America, the better I got at not annoying other road users. Gradually I became road literate through my immersion in the US culture of road use.

In the same way, when we take our first steps into new and unfamiliar environments such as social media, smartphones, or online forum discussions, we need to assimilate into those cultures, which have probably existed long before we grace them with our presence. In texting or email, for example, most people learn that using capital letters is tantamount to shouting.

There are subtler distinctions, such as the use of abbreviations. My 85-year-old father made the mistake of breaking some bad news on Facebook, and supplementing it with a LOL. To him it meant 'lots of love'. To my children it means 'laughing out loud'. It is appropriate for him in his own understanding, but inappropriate and potentially offensive to those already assimilated into the culture of digital communication. I haven't yet asked him what he thinks WTF stands for … welcome to Facebook perhaps?

In summary, skills are essential elements for any practice, but literacies take us beyond the functionality of skills into a deeper level of participation where we begin to appreciate and then adapt our behaviour to the demands and expectations of a new culture. Digital literacies are characterised through the appropriate interpretation and use of digital media and technology. Literacies of this kind are acquired as the learner engages with the culture, mediated through the tools.

If you can't read the signs, how do you know which direction you should go?

Learning 2.0

The phrase Learning 2.0 is a play on Web 2.0, a term coined by Tim O'Reilly to describe the shift from static to participatory Web services. The 'sticky web', where little could be changed, evolved into the 'read/write web', where content could be created and shared, and where social connections were paramount. In came blogs, wikis and social networks, where participation was not only encouraged, it was obligatory. There is a similar argument that a shift has occurred in the way students learn; hence if traditional education was Learning 1.0, then participatory learning enhanced by technology would be Learning 2.0.

The evolution of informal learning from 1.0 to 2.0, from passive to active, from individual to social and from consumer to producer, is represented in our more familiar social web. This shift seems to run parallel to the development of the Web over the last decade, and resonates with many who observe 21st century, digitally mediated forms of learning.

Skills for Learning 2.0

The University of Toronto's Mark Federman is a major contributor to the Learning 2.0 discourse. The writings of Federman's late Canadian compatriot Marshall McLuhan clearly pervade his work. During a live television programme on 21st century learning, Federman was asked whether the traditional three 'R's are still relevant to the present generation of learners. His response was slick and insightful, almost as though it had been scripted well in advance of the TV show (although subsequently Mark has told me it was spontaneous). He declared confidently that for this generation the three 'R's would not be as important as the four 'C's: Connection, Context, Complexity and Connotation. Although each of these are essential characteristics of modern life, it is worth contextualising them appropriately within education as skills and literacies.

Skills for Learning 2.0

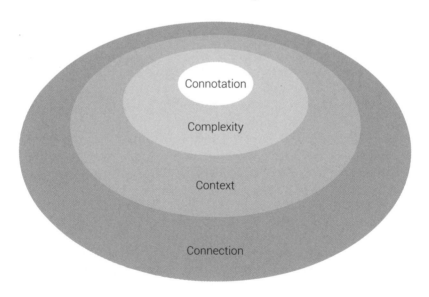

Adapted from: Mark Federman (2012)

Skills for learning 2.0

What follows are my own annotations and thoughts on Federman's framework, illustrated above with a graphic representation.

Firstly, learners need to know how to connect. In today's fast paced and turbulent world, learners need now, like never before, to be able to connect through technology to peers, experts, content and services. One of the most valuable assets 21st century learners own is their personal learning network (PLN). It is not a tangible object or a device. A PLN, as we saw earlier, is a dynamic web of connected minds who share common interests and purposes.

Everyone alive is a 21st century learner, even the many who are not enrolled on an accredited study programme. The majority of their learning each day is informal, and with a powerful enough network of connections to a PLN, there is no limit to what each of us might achieve.

Secondly, learners need to be able to contextualise their learning. Bill Gates once famously declared that content was king. Today, as a tsunami of content overwhelms us, this is no longer the case. Now content is a tyrant and context is king, because situated learning is more powerful, while access to content is just the start of the learning journey. Learning can be contextualised in so many different ways, depending on the needs and perceptions of the individual, and this is why personal learning tools are so important.

The capability to personalise learning environments is vital, as is the ability to exercise agency over the tools and systems you wish to use. The ability to apply learning to one's own individual situation is also an extremely important part of the formula for successful learning today.

Thirdly, today's learners need to be able to work with complexity and be able to correctly interpret content and filter out anything extraneous. They need to be prepared for working in an uncertain future, one which cannot be accurately predicted. In short, students need to be able to see the wood from the trees. They need to be able to quickly interpret a problem and then know how to solve it effectively. There are many tools available today that learners can use to harness the power of Web-based content, including aggregation, curation and tagging tools, all of which can simplify complexity and allow learners to gain a purchase on chaos.

Finally, learners today need to know how to make meaning from the mass of content they are bombarded with each and every day. Many learners do this through discussion, but increasingly we are witnessing a shift toward user-generated content, where learners are creating their own videos, blogs, podcasts, slide sets and other digital artefacts to make meaning.

Txting and all that

I saw a BBC News item about handwriting while I was planning the writing of this book. A member of the public was interviewed in the street about her views on technology and writing. She remarked that 'handwriting is a part of you, and is an expression of your personality, but computer text all looks the same.'

This is true to a certain extent, but computer-generated text also reveals our individuality. Each of us has a 'writing voice' wherein our unique thought processes and idiosyncrasies can be seen. Our ability to adapt to new tools and technologies is a natural human propensity, but often our attempts to transfer from one culture into another can be fraught with difficulties. Those of us who regularly use technology to communicate find occasional difficulties when we misinterpret the nuances of new cultures. Literacy, as Freire[5] once suggested, is not only about reading the word, it is about reading the world. All teachers need digital literacies.

Technoliteracy

For Tim Shortis[6] the term technoliteracy is used to describe how adept a user is in communicating using any given device. For example, SMS texting requires a specific kind of technoliteracy, where the user has to be familiar with a number of features and affordances, including the capabilities (and error issues) of predictive text mode, the 160 character limit per single text, and the multi-function feature of the standard keys on the keypad. They will also need to be aware of the many regularly used colloquial abbreviations, some of which transgress into other modes such as Facebook and email. It encompasses multi-literacies that extend

---

5 Paulo Freire, *Pedagogy of the Oppressed* (London: Bloomsbury Publishing, 2000).
6 Tim Shortis, *The Language of ICT: Information and Communication Technology* (New York: Psychology Press, 2001).

beyond the traditional literacies of reading, writing, speaking and listening. A technoliterate student is able to harness the affordances of new and emerging technologies, using them to communicate in new ways.

Today's students regularly communicate using a large variety of technologies. SMS texts, telephone calls, email, Facebook, Twitter, Snapchat, written language ... the list is quite long, and they definitely use more modes of communication than those that were available to me when I was at university. It therefore follows that they need to learn more forms of literacy than I had to when I was studying for my degree.

I once gave a speech to the University of Chester's final year teacher trainees in which I touched upon the concept of multi-literacy. This was in response to a question from one newly qualified teacher about the potential dumbing down of language through texting. She had heard that texting was encouraging bad spelling and that this might adversely affect students' academic work.

Referred to variously as squeeze text, new literacies, txting, vernacular orthography or unregimented writing,[7] this kind of unorthodox spelling first appeared as a result of the 160 character limit on any single text message. The result was abbreviated spellings, emoticons and phonological representations of orthodox spellings, many of which have since become a part of texting culture. The question thrown at me was about the potential problem of squeeze text spellings appearing in assessed essays and other formal documents. I told her I could see how it could become a problem.

Students in my own programmes occasionally make phonological spelling errors. 'I could of ... ' is a regular mistake I see in the essays I mark. People are beginning to spell as they speak. But it is debatable whether mobile phones are responsible for this. Moreover, we need to ask if this is really a problem if students know which contexts to use these unorthodox spellings in and which to avoid. In 2008 David Crystal[8] related the story of a young student who wrote

---

7 Tim Shortis, *The Language of ICT: Information and Communication Technology* (New York: Psychology Press, 2001).

8 David Crystal, *Txtng: The Gr8 Db8* (Oxford: Oxford University Press, 2008).

an entire essay in squeeze text. One of the lines went something like this:

My smmr hols wr CWOT. B4, we used 2go 2 NY 2C my bro, his GF + thr 3 :-@ kids FTF. ILNY, it's a gr8 plc.

Crystal notes that the actual essay was never tracked down, leading to a fair assumption that the entire story was merely a hoax, and possibly an attempt to sensationalise the issue by the popular press. Regardless of its accuracy or provenance, the press had a field day, and a storm of protests ensued. Crystal, a globally acknowledged expert on language, was less moved, and suggested that regardless of the strange appearance (or morphology) of the words, they nevertheless followed orthodox grammatical structure. He wryly remarked that for sheer creativity, he would have awarded the student 10 out of 10, but for appropriateness, 0 out of 10.

Crystal and others make the point that language is evolving and new words are appearing all the time in the English language (in all its many forms worldwide), because language is organic and the culture it emerges from is constantly adapting to change, as are the meanings of some words.

There is a new ethos now. Languages are becoming more fluid where new vocabulary and alternative spellings are continually added. We need to question whether the controversy of squeeze text is really as serious an issue as some suggest, or whether there is more than a hint of hyperbole and hysteria about the 'dumbing down' of the English language.

My response to the newly qualified teacher's question was to point out that today's students are able to adapt their writing according to the various media they use to communicate. Being habituated to using a particular medium, the students assimilate the culture of that particular tool and communicate appropriately within it. In many ways this is akin to living and working in a foreign country, when to survive and be inconspicuous one learns to adopt the practices and social mores of the host country in parallel to learning the new language.

This transcends skill and becomes a literacy. Students generally know the difference between communicating in SMS and writing a formal essay, and will usually follow the rules.

Transliteracy

Another important development in the study of digital literacies is transliteracy. Transliteracy can be defined as being literate across a number of platforms. In essence, it is the ability to be able to create content, organise, share and communicate through a variety of social media, discussion groups, mobile tools and other services that are commonly available. It is being able to articulate your ideas equally powerfully in a variety of available contexts, whether it is face to face or via telephone, video, audio or text.

This assumes that the nuances of our communication can vary depending on the tool we use. When I teach in a co-present context (face to face), it is qualitatively different for me and my students from a remote webinar style presentation I might give through Blackboard Collaborate or Adobe Connect. It's not just the experience – I also behave differently, and manage my impression in a different way. I have argued in previous publications that the way we represent ourselves (using avatars, user names, etc.) varies for many depending on what medium we are using. People represent themselves differently in Second Life to the way they represent themselves on Facebook, because the affordances of each environment prompt a different response from them.

On LinkedIn I manage a professional version of my online persona, which evaporates when I'm on Facebook. On Twitter I can be a bit of a mixture. Sometimes I like to have a bit of fun and at other times I'm deadly serious. I have also discussed the idea that each tool has its own particular set of affordances which enable or constrain particular ways of using it. However, although these tools are different they all have a common purpose. Thomas et al. express this very well:

> From early signing and orality through handwriting, print, TV and film to networked digital media, the concept of transliteracy calls for a change of perspective away from the battles over print versus digital, and a move instead towards a unifying ecology not just of media, but of all literacies relevant to reading, writing, interaction and culture, both past and present. It is, we hope, an opportunity to cross some very obstructive divides.[9]

---

9 S. Thomas, C. Joseph, J. Lacetti, B. Mason, B. S. Mills, S. Perril and K. Pullinger, 'Transliteracy: Crossing Divides', *First Monday* 12 (2007): 3.

So for Thomas et al. the argument over whether media are different – for example, whether digital will replace paper – is spurious. It's more important for us to recognise the significance of each tool, and how they can be used effectively in all their variations, and also in combinations. Ultimately, transliteracy should be about using whatever media and communication tools are at our disposal, and also being able to discern which tools will be the most effective and appropriate in any given context. Do we learn better watching a YouTube video or reading a text? Are we better at presenting our ideas in pictures or as a podcast? I know my answer to that, and it may be different to your answer – we all learn differently.

It's also the reason they are likely to choose Facebook rather than the institutional email system when they want to send each other messages. But students do use all of these tools, and it is important to ensure that they are comfortable with each and have the requisite skills to exploit each tool to its optimum value. This is why transliteracy is becoming increasingly important as a digital literacy. It will assume even more significance as more of us become our own broadcasters, publishers and directors.

Keeping safe online

Earlier in the book I argued that although numerous threats and risks emerge when children use technology, teachers should be aware that this is a problem that is inherent in society rather than in the technology. When I was speaking at an event in New Zealand, during the question time a principal of one of the local schools declared that he had banned the use of the Internet in his school because it was dangerous. I asked him if he had also stopped teaching children how to cross the road, because that was dangerous too.

What better place is there to teach children how to use the Internet safely than a school? The knee-jerk reactions of education leaders to ban or exclude any technology from the learning space because it might pose a danger to students is a huge mistake. Not only do decisions of this kind disadvantage children while they are in school, it also sends them a message that the technologies they use outside of school are not relevant to learning. Worse, it is likely that their use of technology outside of school will be more of a risk because they have received no formal learning on how to use mobile phones and the Internet safely and with consideration. Teachers can and should teach digital literacies, and e-safety is one of the most important areas that schools should consider including in their curricula.

Students of all ages need to be keenly aware of the dangers of cyberbullying, inadvertent disclosure of personal details, damage to reputation and the other negative impacts on their lives that can result from complacent use of technology. A salutary tale of woe that could not have been anticipated was related in a chapter I wrote with Helen Keegan. It featured the story of Star Wars Kid, a story that has come to epitomise digital privacy, offering a lesson we can all learn from. Here's an adapted excerpt from the chapter:

Star Wars Kid

In 2002, a slightly overweight and bespectacled Canadian teenager recorded a video of himself clumsily but energetically swinging a wooden pole around his head, in homage to the Darth Maul character from the Star Wars film The Phantom Menace. He recorded the tape in his high school studio, and then it was left forgotten in a school store room. One day a classmate found it, viewed it, and considered that it was amusing enough to share with his friends. Between them they made several copies, and eventually the clip was uploaded as a file onto the Internet. Ultimately, it found its way onto YouTube. The video then spread rapidly and virally, through friends telling friends, sending links, texts, and via the sharing of files.

Within a few weeks the video had been downloaded and viewed by several million others. Soon alternative versions began to appear on YouTube and elsewhere on the Web; some with cleverly overdubbed music and sound effects, others parodying Star Wars, and then other popular movies such as The Matrix. Some versions were embellished with sophisticated visual effects, spectacular glowing lightsaber overlays and other editing tricks, so that an entire suite of 'Star Wars Kid' videos was made available for viewing online.

It is estimated that collectively, the various versions of the Star Wars Kid video clips have been downloaded over a billion times, predominantly from YouTube. Several versions of the clip have even found their way onto mainstream broadcast television. But most viewers of the video, while chuckling to themselves at the absurdity of its content, fail to realise that someone was hurt and humiliated by it. Ultimately, the teenage boy's unsought Internet and television publicity led to prolonged embarrassment and exposure to harassment and mockery that became unbearable to him. He was reported to have undergone long term psychiatric care. In 2006, the Associated Sun Press reported that the boy's family had successfully reached an out-of-court settlement with the families of his classmates for a sum of $350,000 Canadian dollars.[10]

This is just one of a number of similar sad tales that have emerged in recent years related directly to the misuse and abuse of digital media. All users should be made aware of their vulnerability to these issues, and the risks involved every time they venture online. e-safety, including digital privacy, should be a key component in any form of digital literacy education

---

10 Steve Wheeler and Helen Keegan, 'Imagined Worlds, Emerging Cultures', in S. Wheeler (ed.), *Connected Minds, Emerging Cultures* (Charlotte NC: Information Age, 2009), p. 266.

13

Digital Identities

We know what we are, but not what we may be.

William Shakespeare

Who are you? How do you let other people know who you are? Are you the same person online as you are in real life? Can you separate your professional identity from your personal identity?

These questions show that the concept of personal identity is complex. Perpetually, there seem to be discussions around identity on popular social media channels. Twitter can be a particularly powerful forum for such dialogue, as it proved once again when I tweeted several questions around this topic. There ensued a protracted and captivating conversation between several members of my PLN, and some of the responses and conversations are reported here in this chapter.

I asked if professional identity can be separated from personal identity. One response was from David Hopkins at Leicester University who thought it was entirely possible, but suggested that 'adding a personal touch, you become a personality where background and experience can enhance professional impact' – so perhaps it may be useful if the identities can inform each other. Guido Gautsch, a teacher in Melbourne agreed, but argued that it was probably not possible to separate them on open social media platforms such as Twitter. Jon Kruithof at McMaster University also concurred, but with the caveat that it depends on what you share and the groups you share with. 'The more you share, the less likely you will keep them separated,' he remarked, invoking the idea of PLNs (personal learning networks).

At Reading University, Pat Parslow thought that separation between personal and professional identities had to occur, and saw a social dimension, asking whether PLNs were 'built, uncovered, grown or nurtured'. In response, I suggested that all four were possible, depending on who we are and what weight we place on our PLNs. Many professionals manage two separate accounts to try to differentiate between their professional and personal (or less formal) personae.

Some educators such as Jane Davis at Colchester Institute said they thought it was a good idea to do this to maintain salience and focus on context specific roles, but others such as technology commentator Martin King at the Royal Holloway in London saw problems, suggesting that 'just as identity is complex, so is trying to divide it'.

The common consensus was that personal identity is a more or less constant concept, but that elements of it can change depending on context.

The phenomenal growth in popularity of self-broadcasting and publishing through social media raises some new questions about how people represent themselves in virtual spaces. Sherry Turkle[1] was one of the first people to conduct detailed studies in this area, observing behaviour in multiple user domains (MUDs) for her book *Life on Screen*. Writing in 1995, as the first crest of the Web broke onto our collective consciousness, Turkle revealed how many people employ multiple identities in virtual worlds. She showed that in some cases these virtual representations of ourselves can become as real to people as their identity in 'real life'. These studies led Turkle to propose that new forms of personal identity are emerging as a result of prolonged interaction with others through technology – that our identities are increasingly multiple and decentred.

So 'we are who we are', each of us unique individuals. Yet it seems that context and other variables can change this, at least temporarily, creating a kind of fluid identity set that switches between contexts. This is very much aligned with Erving Goffman's drama model,[2] in which he suggested that we adopt front stage (public) and backstage (private) roles depending on where we find ourselves located across the formal-informal spectrum of our daily activities. We will explore this theory in a little more depth in the next section of this chapter.

---

1 Sherry Turkle, *Life on Screen: Identity in the Age of the Internet* (Simon & Schuster, 1995).

2 Erving Goffman, 'Role-distance', in Brisset, D. and Edgley, C. (eds.) *Life as Theater: A Dramaturgical Sourcebook,* (Chicago: Aldine Publishing Company, 1961): 123–132.

This continuum of identities – or versions of it – was an idea that several argued for in the Twitter discussion.

Identity in online environments tends to be even more difficult to express for some. When asked how online identity might be defined, Aaron Davis, a teacher in Melbourne, Australia said his identity was 'complicated, contradictory and complex. Ever evolving, yet also staying the same.' An interesting response came from Rev. Sally Jones, a priest in the UK who said that it was 'me, but 10% better', to which I responded by asking whether she found some added value through the affordances of the tool she used. She replied that she used social media for work and it gave her the chance to 'think things through properly before acting'. It is often this kind of 'reflection time' that prevents us from saying what we think immediately, and enables us to better represent ourselves and our ideas in a more considered way. This could be seen as a kind of identity regulation through asynchronous filtering.

José Picardo, an assistant principal at a school in England said that his identity was managed, adding: 'If I don't manage it, someone else will', acknowledging the potential of outside social influences to impact negatively upon one's reputation. Finally, Helen Blunden, another teacher from Melbourne, Australia revealed how complex and confused she thought her online identity could be when she said it was: 'Same but different. Online, mindful but more expressive; cautious but also creative; guarded yet open and sharing. Confused.'

The drama of Facebook

Facebook is a social phenomenon that cannot be ignored. The diverse behaviours witnessed on the site are just one of the many features that provoke great interest from psychologists and social anthropologists. Building on the early work of Turkle, many ethnographic studies have already been conducted into Facebook's impact on relationships, social movements, self-concept and digital identity.

Erving Goffman certainly would have had a lot to say about social networks and personal identity if he had lived to see their counterplay, so permit me to indulge in one final flight of fancy as I speculate on what Goffman might have said about Facebook.

Goffman is well known for work on psychiatric asylums, social rituals and stigma, but perhaps his best known work is his dramaturgical model of human interaction. Developing his theory, Goffman's thinking was probably influenced by symbolic interactionists such as George Herbert Mead and Charles Cooley, and sociologists such as Émile Durkheim and Talcott Parsons. In his model Goffman argued that each of us 'manage our impression' when we find ourselves in the presence of others.

For Goffman, human behaviour was very much dependent on time, space and audience. By audience, he meant those who are observing the actor, or with whom s/he interacts. In essence, Goffman argued that the way each of us presents ourselves to others is carefully managed around the cultural values, norms and expectations that are commonly held by actor and audience. Watch how comedians, stage actors, pop singers, and even politicians manipulate their audiences and you will see how much they desire to be liked, accepted and paid attention to.

Front stage, backstage

Developing the drama metaphor, Goffman proposed that each of us has a 'front stage', where we are at our most guarded, and present ourselves according to prevailing cultural norms, values and expectations. Goffman's notion of impression management evokes the construction of the self simultaneously in the mind of the individual and also in the collective minds of the audience. We see ourselves reflected in the eyes of others and then try to adjust our behaviour to conform and to remain acceptable to those with whom we choose to relate.[3] It is a kind of 'performance', where we conceal what we consider to be unpleasant or undesirable aspects of our personae whilst emphasising desirable and more attractive attributes to our 'audience' of others.

This is also the region within which we adopt roles and subsequently perform specific mannerisms, follow scripts and project a controlled appearance that may be further enhanced with props and costumes. According to Goffman, the way people 'manage their impression' in the presence of others involves some kind of role playing (self-

---

3   Charles Cooley, *Human Nature and the Social Order* (New York: Scribner, 1902).

representation) and can also involve scripts (speech patterns), props and costumes, just as an actor does for a stage performance. Such management of impression is common to all humans and is used to form relationships and gain influence with others.

Conversely, the 'backstage' region is where we are less guarded and more relaxed, and reveal a more natural representation of ourselves. This is usually a more honest persona, where we let our hair down and step out of the character we may have adopted in our front stage, formal roles. The backstage is a space seemingly devoid of an audience, and an area where the individual might feel able to relax into a more authentic, less contrived persona.

Facebook users may feel that they are at home and relaxed when they are online, and 'among friends'. Maybe it is perceived by them as a backstage area where they can relax after a hard day at the office. Nevertheless, they are performing a role, and are unwittingly engaging with an audience of others.

Because Facebook is generally a public space that can be manipulated and 'controlled' by privacy settings, many Facebook users may indeed be in a more private space with their 'friends'. Many, however, are largely ignorant of the privacy controls and unknowingly leave themselves open to observation from 'outsiders'. They thus fail to manage their impression effectively in this front stage region, because they assume that they are located within a backstage region.

This may be one explanation why people appear to be less guarded on social media, and feel free to say things they would never dream of saying in a real-life public space. The incongruence – in Goffman's terms – of someone adopting a backstage, relaxed role whilst unknowingly appearing in a front stage area can have disastrous consequences upon their self-concept, or their reputation.

Friends and others who may have access to the user's personal artefacts, such as text information, conversations, pictures and videos, have the ability to publish these more widely than the user might be comfortable with. Their content, devised in and for a backstage context, is suddenly thrust into the limelight of a front stage region. Images of users that were intended solely for private use might be reposted to wider circles of 'friends of friends' without the subject's permission, and then the horrified individual has to request that that image be removed. They find themselves thrust into a front stage position against their will, and are then at the mercy of the person who posted the image. Indeed, many relationships have been damaged or fractured because of such actions.

Worse, some of the more vulnerable users who have become victims of cyberbullying and blackmail have tragically taken their own lives.[4] Those who fall foul of the trap of thinking they are acting in a private, backstage space also discover the dangers of unguarded moments, when they are dismissed from their jobs or their reputation is tarnished.

For many, the drama of Facebook is very real.

Digital me, digital you

Increasingly, as we spend more of our time online, we are creating, repurposing, sharing, searching and consuming content and communicating with others. All of these activities leave behind a tangible trail, a digital footprint, a record of where we have been and what we have done. More significantly, in psychological terms, each of us is developing a personal digital presence, and continually modifying our digital profiles. These are some of the essential elements that constitute an individual's digital identity – who we are in a variety of contexts in digital environments and how we present ourselves and manage our impressions in our digital lives.

A useful model to aid our understanding of the interaction between individuals, tools and technologies, other people and the wider learning ecosystem, is one developed by Engeström[5] and his colleagues, which we now know as second-generation Activity Theory.

My interpretation of digital identity is shown in the figure below, overlaid against the original model. I have used it to describe the essential elements and actions that might help to build one's digital identity.

---

4 Harriet Arkell, 'Coroner Warns of Dangers of Facebook', Mail Online. Available online at: http://www.dailymail.co.uk/news/article-2513782/Facebook-bullies-led-suicide-student-19-hanged-himself.html.
5 Yrjö Engeström, 'Activity Theory and Individual and Social Transformation', *Perspectives on Activity Theory* (1999): 19–38.

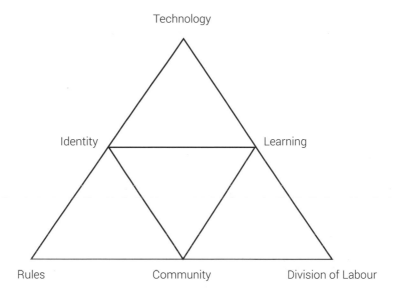

Clearly, any discussion of digital identity is a complex proposition. The relationship between identity and the other elements in the Activity Theory model is not as clear cut as the diagram might have us believe. Below is an annotated version of the Activity model with theoretical implications indicated for all of the relationships between components.

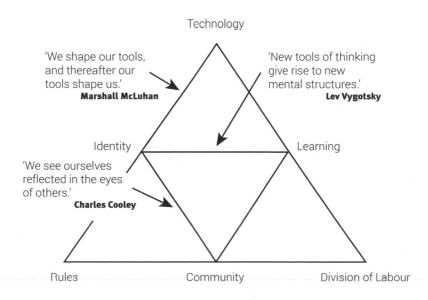

I found it useful to apply statements by leading theorists to depict a few of the pathways and relationships within the model. For example, Marshall McLuhan[6] made specific reference to the relationship between people and technology when he declared, 'We shape our tools, and then our tools shape us.' The symbolic interactionist theorist Charles Cooley saw the impact of community upon the behaviour of individuals when he wrote, 'We see ourselves reflected in the eyes of others.' Vygotsky's observation that 'new tools of thinking give rise to new mental structures' resonates particularly in relation to learning, identity and technology.

From the above it is clear that identity can be influenced and even manipulated by technology. Technology can be used to portray the self in many different ways, transform the self-concept and even extend one's identity into contexts beyond normal physical capabilities. Technology can strongly influence the way we perceive ourselves, enabling us to transcend our own limitations as we invest our energies and time. Technology, in McLuhan's terms, is very much an extension of the human and, we might also claim, of human identity. These characteristics of technology use and their potential impact on the user have become the focus of research.

Lost in the crowd?

In his book *Distraction*, Mark Curtis[7] argues that our sense of self – or personal identity – can become confused or challenged when we habitually use digital technology. He makes several salient points about the blurring of boundaries between public and private (think, for example, of complacent use of webcams and Facebook status updates) and believes that technology tends to distract us from 'who we are'. There has been debate over whether or not people should combine their personal and business identities on social media. Several colleagues have told me they keep separate personal and professional accounts.

---

6   Marshall McLuhan, *Understanding Media: The Extensions of Man* (Chicago: MIT Press, 1994).
7   Mark Curtis, *Distraction: Being Human in the Digital Age* (London: Futuretext, 2004).

Curtis argues from the position that identity is malleable rather than fixed, and that we learn from a very early age that we can be someone else through role playing, imagination or masquerade. Our immersion in media, he argues, provides us with a myriad of alternative role models we can adopt or adapt. By the same token, social media also give us endless opportunities to engage with others, including sports stars, entertainers, politicians and other celebrities.

The Curtis position is that other people's lives are more glamorous than our own, and therefore we wish we could be them to escape from the mundane, if only for a while. All very well, but I'm not convinced that this argument is applicable to everyone. Does wishing to be someone else mean that you actually adopt their identity? It's highly unlikely.

Curtis also seems to be implying that people are often unwilling or at least unconscious participants in the digital obfuscation of their identities. Again, this is a far from convincing argument, but even if it were true, would it really be so much of a bad thing that we are able to engage in multiple online identity performances? What dangers might there be? Also, do we really find ourselves forced into performing multiple identities against our will?

Personally speaking

Those who subscribe to my blog or follow my Twitter accounts will know that I am very willing to experiment with multiple identities because I am fascinated by the new possibilities and intrigued by the psychology behind personal use of social media. However, it should be stressed that I engage with this through choice, and I feel fully in control of what is posted on these channels. To the amusement of my network of friends, I sometimes hold conversations and contrive arguments between my @timbuckteeth and @stevewheeler Twitter accounts, as though the two are separate personalities. In reality, I see myself exploiting the affordances of multiple accounts to explore the possibilities of dialogue and polemic around interesting issues. Does this mean I have two identities? Is my true identity being lost as a result of this unusual dialogue? This is a question that is often explored. I once discussed the question of identity loss due to globalisation when I wrote the following:

> There is an argument that due to the process of globalisation, national boundaries (and therefore tribal boundaries) have been eroded to the point that we are amalgamating into a homogenous mass of humanity, and where the last vestiges of tribal identity are vanishing. In essence, the forces of globalisation have amalgamated us all into one tribe. We are living in a 'corporate age', runs the argument, in which all our decisions are being dictated by 'those who have the real power'. Thus, whenever I travel, I can find the same fast food outlets and the same familiar chain stores where I can purchase clothing and footwear I will be comfortable wearing. I can blend into the background because I am wearing a similar style of clothing to the hundreds of other people milling around in the high street, and I will not be conspicuous, because I am eating the same food and drinking from an identical soft drink can as the natives. Have I therefore blended in to such an extent into the local culture that I have lost my identity? No, my identity remains intact, while my individuality is subsumed into the melange within which I am located. Identity and individualism are not synonymous, even though there are obvious commonalities.[8]

I would conclude that personal identity can be blurred or disguised, but it remains essentially intact. Immersion in virtual social worlds such as Second Life are also contexts where we can blur the boundaries of identity. Mark Curtis makes a useful point that in such environments users don't necessarily know the people they are interacting with, because they often hide behind pseudonyms and always represent themselves as avatars.

This does not necessarily mean that one's identity is being changed or that users 'lose control' of who they are, though it may mean that people open themselves up to identity theft or manipulation of their public-facing image by others. Mark Curtis[9] also makes a useful point that managing multiple identities can demand a lot of effort and therefore become a distraction. I have discovered the effects of this personally, because I maintain six different Twitter accounts. I therefore need to be very careful – especially when using platforms such as TweetDeck – that I check carefully which account I'm using before I hit the send button.

---

8   Steve Wheeler, 'Digital Tribes, Virtual Clans', in S. Wheeler (ed.), *Connected Minds, Emerging Cultures* (Charlotte NC: Information Age, 2009): 65–76.
9   Mark Curtis, *Distraction: Being Human in the Digital Age* (London: Futuretext, 2004).

Distributed digital identity

In the future, as digital spaces multiply and technology continues to evolve, each of us will have opportunities to inhabit as many virtual worlds and adopt as many personae as we wish, and yet remain one person. People will be able to form new versions of their identity in a variety of different cyberspaces, and project these identities diversely. Selfies and simple avatars are merely the beginning of this digital identity representation, transformation and distribution. Along with the idea of the quantified self,[10] the concept of distributed digital identity has the potential to be transformational and liberating.

On the other hand it could also be calamitous for our sense of community, society, and for our collective mental health.

The advances being made in bioengineering, robotics, artificial intelligence and nanotechnology – our transhumanist futures[11] – can play out in many ways. We have yet to see what specific contributions any of these might make to our educational futures.

Once, where traditional education was the only option, learners had to be co-present with their teachers. Then along came various forms of distance education, where learner and teacher were separated by geographical distance and conversation was mediated through technology. Blended forms of traditional and remote education followed. We now find ourselves in a transitionary phase where we are just beginning to come to terms with the ways technology might mediate our virtual, social and cognitive presence in synchronous and asynchronous spaces.

The recent rapid advances in connecting infrastructures, processing speed and mobile, wearable interfaces could lead to a bewildering array of future pedagogical possibilities. Some of these might enhance and enrich our future learning experiences, but some may be accompanied by serious risks we have not yet begun to consider.

---

10 Steve Wheeler, 'A Day in the Life: The Quantified Self', Learning with 'e's (2014). Available online at: http://steve-wheeler.blogspot.co.uk/2014/02/a-day-in-life-quantified-self.html.

11 Steve Wheeler, 'GRIN and Bear it: Our Transhumanist Futures', Learning with 'e's (2014). Available online at: http://steve-wheeler.blogspot.co.uk/2013/06/grin-and-bear-it.html.

When we are liberated from our physical and temporal constraints everything becomes possible, but not everything is desirable. The final chapter explores these and other thoughts and ideas about the future of learning.

14 The Shape of Minds to Come

The only way we can begin to think about our possible futures is to take a leap of imagination outside and beyond.

Arthur C. Clarke

When I try to gaze into the future it hurts my eyes. It's impossible to predict the future. On a visit to Las Vegas I went to one of the many casinos and gazed around at a huge space filled with ingenious ways to win and lose money. I knew that if I could predict the future, I would become a millionaire overnight. But as I don't gamble I sat and watched, fascinated, as other people tried to predict the future.

Most of them lost their money.

I'm not a prophet or a clairvoyant. I have no special powers for predicting the future. And yet I receive a constant flow of invitations to speak about the future of learning. It's an interesting time to be involved in the future business. Certain physicists are now arguing that the present, the past and the future are much the same thing, but they tend to use complex formulae and obfuscate their arguments with strange phrases such as string theory, virtual particles and quantum mechanics. For the rest of us, the reality is that the past is a memory and the future is imaginary.

All we have and experience is anchored in the present; time flows in a straight line, and it only flows in one direction.

Old technology and emerging trends

One way to discover what is on the horizon is to examine the past to see what lies there, to see where we have come from. But even this can be fraught with difficulty. Many technologies are a lot older than we realise. The fax machine is 150 years old (in 1846 it was called the telecopier). Newer technologies such as the tablet computer and mobile telephone were first conceived in the sixties.

Another way is to look at current trends, but this can be just as problematic. Many emerging technologies are already on the drawing board or in production before we ever see them appearing in science fiction movies. Gesture-based computing was already being developed before it featured in the movie *Minority Report*. While he was researching for the film, director Steven Spielberg visited MIT to see a prototype being demonstrated. He liked the idea so much he included it in one of the opening sequences of his movie.

There are times when these emerging ideas and prototype technologies help us to anticipate what might be the possibilities for education. We could tell in the late eighties that multimedia was going to be very big. And so it was. In the late nineties, with the new millennium approaching, we could see that everything was beginning to converge on the Web. Online learning exploded in popularity.

Several years ago, while speaking at a major conference, I stuck my head above the parapet and predicted that the future of learning would be built on the use of smartphone technology. I was fortunate to be fairly accurate with my prediction, but it wasn't really that much of a risk – mobile phones were penetrating into just about every aspect of our lives.

Where the technology goes, it seems education eventually has to follow. How quickly it follows depends on the vision and willingness of educators.

Tunnel vision

Some predictions of the future are often seen as ludicrous in hindsight, especially if they are quite specific. Where are all the flying cars and moon colonies? Whatever happened to personal jet packs and underwater cities? These were romantic visions of the future but they never came to fruition. Predictions about the future are often wide of the mark because we talk about the future from our limited present-time horizons. Alexander Graham Bell, credited with inventing the telephone, once declared: 'I truly believe that one day, there will be a telephone in every city in America.'

He was right. There is.

Unfortunately, Bell was only gazing down a very narrow corridor of time. One thing he wasn't able to foresee was how small and agile and affordable telephones would become. Because his knowledge was limited to his own time and place, he couldn't see clearly enough into the future to predict miniaturisation, satellite networks and touchscreens. He wasn't aware that one day each of us would carry a telephone in our pockets. Our future vision is often narrow, based upon our limited knowledge and rooted in our present experience.

Our personal cultures and limited frame of reference also constrain our vision. While on a train journey recently, I overheard a conversation between two young school boys. One was saying how much he liked the new *Sherlock* TV series, starring Benedict Cumberbatch and Martin Freeman. His friend agreed, but sagely pointed out that the 'classic' Sherlock Holmes films were far superior – the ones starring Robert Downey Jr. and Jude Law! The boys were unaware that the work of Sir Arthur Conan Doyle had spawned a much longer movie history, and to them 'classic' meant something entirely different to those who had lived a little longer.

The only way we can ever begin to think about our possible futures is to take a leap of imagination outside and beyond our current knowledge and experiences. That is a very difficult thing to do when you don't know what you don't know.

Inventing our future

Recently I was invited onto a TV news programme to be interviewed about new technology in schools. One of the schools in my area had dipped into its budget and had purchased a touchscreen tablet computer for every one of the children. The decision polarised the public, and generated quite a lot of media interest.

The TV interviewer's first question was, 'Is this the future of education?' My response was, 'No, it's the present. And in a few years' time, your children are going to ask you, "Mum, did you really have to touch a computer to make it work?"'

Technology is rapidly advancing but we only see what we have now, and think 'isn't this magical?' Time moves on, but often we stay rooted to the spot, content in the present. We must be prepared for the future, whatever it may hold (although that's easier said than done). The future may very well include wearable technology and computers that are activated by gesture and voice. But what form will they take, and how much will they affect our lives?

We can either allow the future to happen to us or we can invent our own futures. To do so, we need to stop thinking about the future from our current perspective, and as Arthur C. Clarke recommended, take some leaps of imagination into the seemingly impossible. Such thinking should not be restricted to science fiction writers; this calls for some creative thinking and invention on the part of educators too. If we are to invent our own futures, we need to step outside our own frames of reference and begin to conceive of new forms of education that currently do not exist, and at present may not seem possible.

We need to be free to *imagine*. Teachers need latitude to be able to innovate. Innovation is being able to do something different and better, not just with what we have, but also with what is coming. That means educators need to keep an eye on the horizon for new tools and methods. This may sound a little paradoxical, but for teachers there is probably no better place to start a journey of imagination than the place with which they are most familiar: the traditional classroom.

The future of classrooms

The classroom has been the focal point of education for many generations. Universities have been referred to as 'seats of learning' for centuries. Education has long been situated in specific locations and those locations are often exclusive, closed to outsiders. Now a trend that has been gathering pace for the last decade is signalling movement away from traditional learning environments towards the opening up of education. Wherever education is conducted, it is likely that future provision will be less closed and exclusive. It is conceivable that schools of the future will be more open, connecting with other schools and with their communities on an open basis, sharing their content more freely. Social media will make this happen.

Many universities, too, will be forced to open their courses to outsiders. This is a trend that has already gained significant global momentum through the MOOC movement, and in such initiatives as the Open Education Resources (OER) University and WikiEducator.

With the proliferation of open universities, technology supported learning and open education, many would argue that the classroom is no longer the centre for education. Others would argue that technologies such as personal devices and social media channels such as YouTube have made informal learning accessible to all. Still others would point out that schools, colleges and universities are still there, as numerous as ever, and are showing little sign of decline.

Traditionally, learning has been conducted in classrooms or lecture halls where the presence of an expert or specialist in a subject takes to the stage and delivers knowledge directly to the assembled students. The didactic method is cost-effective in terms of the amount of contact time lecturers or teachers need to invest in the process. The student is then left to think and reflect on the knowledge they have 'received' and eventually, is assessed on how well they can remember, apply and evaluate this knowledge.

Classroom centric education has established itself as a 'tried and tested' method of pedagogy, and it doesn't seem to be waning. Many mainstream organisations continue to practise this approach, and educational institutions everywhere continue to build classrooms and lecture halls along the same design. Although the didactic method has been severely criticised as less effective than more active and participatory pedagogies, it persists.

The future of intelligence

Many commentators express concern about the negative impact technology may have on our ability to think critically, construct knowledge and read/research more deeply. As we saw in Chapter 3, their primary argument is that we are becoming increasingly dependent on search engines and other tools that trivialise knowledge and simplify what we learn.

A secondary argument is that there is a large amount of content on the Web that is spurious, deceptive or inaccurate and that user-generated content such as Wikipedia and blogs undermines the authority of professionals and academics.

Futurologist Ray Kurzweil sees beyond these issues, believing that mobile computing actually enables us to increase our cognitive abilities. He argues that we are becoming more creative in our learning and have developed the potential for endless cognitive gain as a result of sustained access to these technologies. His position is reminiscent of the work of American cognitive psychologist David Jonassen and his colleagues,[1] who proposed that computers could serve as mind tools. As was highlighted in Chapter 3, technology can amplify our cognitive abilities and expand our memories. They become natural extensions of our capabilities.

Other commentators, such as Karen Stephenson, believe that we store our knowledge with our friends, and that connected peer networks are where learning occurs in the digital age. British computer scientist and philosopher Andy Clark is of the opinion that we are all naturally aligned to using technology. In his seminal work, *Natural Born Cyborgs*,[2] Clark sees a future that combines the

---

1   David H. Jonassen, Kyle Peck and Brett Wilson, *Learning with Technology: A Constructivist Perspective* (Under Saddle River: Merrill Prentice Hall, 1999).
2   Andy Clark, *Natural Born Cyborgs: Minds, Technologies and the Future of Human Intelligence* (Oxford: Oxford University Press, 2003).

best features of human and machine, where we literally wear or physically internalise our technologies. Physicist Michio Kaku holds a similar opinion, predicting that one day even our contact lenses will be connected to the Web.

There are examples of how such cyborg existence might come about, and they are not too far in the distance. Recently, demonstrations of Google Glass (eyewear that connects you via augmented reality software and gestural control to information beyond your normal visual experience) and Muse (a brainwave-sensing headband) have veered us in the direction of cyborg experience. Also announced at the time of writing is a contact lens that monitors its wearer for diabetes and other illnesses. Many are predicting that other devices – wearable, natural gesture based, and sensor rich – will appear in the next few years, and these will be affordable to many.

Divided we fall

Writer William Gibson once said, the future may be here already, but it's just not evenly distributed. There is a truth in this. A persistent digital divide does exist between the industrialised world and emerging countries. Mobile phones may be proliferating rapidly in some areas but they are less evident in others. This is not simply a division between the rich and the poor – digital divides also exist within Western society of a psychological rather than socio-economic nature. There is a whole spectrum of alternative personal responses to technology in every population, from wildly enthusiastic to outright rejection.

There are further divides between those who can use the technologies and those who can't. Technology remains unevenly distributed, and will be for some time to come. But the digital divide will not stop the march of technology. The next stage in our ongoing romance with technology will be more intimate, when we begin to wear our devices.

Many have asked what wearables and natural gesture interfaces achieve for us. We are not certain, for example, whether wearable technologies will increase our intelligence, but it doesn't stop us speculating. What such tools *will* be able to do is free us up physically, enhancing our visual capabilities and enabling us to control devices hands-free. They will also enable us to free up cognitive resources by distributing our thinking and extending our memories, enabling us to focus on salient thought processes such as creativity, intuitive thinking and critical reflection and, of course, managing our personal relationships.

Our wearable computers will navigate, search, discover, store, retrieve, organise and connect for us. It is doubtful these tools will make us any smarter, but they may enable us to behave smarter, work smarter and learn smarter. That is contingent, of course, on our acceptance that the success or failure of such tools is ultimately down to us and us alone. Winning hearts and minds will make the difference between success and failure in any organisation.

The future of human—computer interaction

We may be approaching a point in our human development where our relationship with our technologies becomes so natural that they actually become a part of us. The current generation of students are already demonstrating an element of psychological dependency on smartphones. The next generation of technologies may be even more seductive in their power, enabling us to perform tasks that were previously inconceivable. They will extend our minds and physical capabilities further than we ever thought possible. We need to be aware that change is no longer linear – now it is exponential. At present our technologies and digital tools are predominantly external to our bodies, but I believe that will change.

Will we ever be able to claim that technologies are a viable extension of our physical capabilities, seamlessly connected to our minds?

Perhaps the first part of the above question would have been easier to answer in the last century than it is today. The answer then would have been 'yes – we have already achieved it.' The widespread use of diverse technologies such as transportation vehicles, the telegraph, manufacturing tools, weapons and even writing implements, demonstrated that we can create technology to extend our abilities beyond our natural physical skills, and also adapt our bodies and minds to incorporate tools. This is an effect epitomised in Marshall

McLuhan's famous declaration that 'we shape our tools, and thereafter our tools shape us'.

Although this has social and cultural connotations it also reveals that we are naturally pliable, and can adapt our personal skills and expectations, and especially our neurological systems, towards new and unfamiliar ways of doing things. In this case, we learn to use our tools to extend and strengthen our limited physical capabilities.

A moveable feast

The second part of the question – whether technology can ever be connected seamlessly to our minds – poses a problem. Setting aside ethical issues, and whether we actually wish to be seamlessly interfaced with technology, there are doubts over feasibility. As our tools become increasingly complex, so arises a need to learn more complex skills to be able to optimise our use of those tools.

The computer is a classic example of a simple technology that can be perceived as overly complex and difficult to use.

Things have dramatically improved since the early days of Graphic User Interfaces, and Siri and Kinect have helped to bring us a little closer to improved voice, facial and natural gesture control. But the problem remains that as computers exponentially increase in power and utility, and new functionality is added, we will always need to run just to keep up with their development. Most of us fail to harness the full potential of digital technology because we simply don't have the skills or the time to exploit its possibilities.

Our previously learnt skills are so practised that they become unconscious competencies but these are of little value when we transgress into unfamiliar, alien environments. We then need to be able to adapt our old skills and competencies to our new culture. Digital environments are alien environments, so it follows we need new literacies in the use of technology before we can reap its benefits. This will take up a considerable amount of our time and energy.

The future of teaching

What will the future hold for teaching? I firmly believe there will be a place for teachers in the future because they provide the inspiration learners need to succeed. No amount of technology, self-study or user-generated content can ever replace a good teacher. Educators will still be there to motivate and give impetus, and they will act as pedagogy experts to facilitate and support quality learning. What they will surely do less of is 'teach'. There will need to be less 'front of the classroom' activities and more drawing alongside learners in project work, small group activities, problem-based learning and technology-enhanced processes. Most importantly, teachers will need to work more in partnership with their students as co-learners.

In the future, we will need to prepare for the eventuality that teachers may not be physically present in some classrooms. Instead, they may adopt a virtual presence, particularly in places that are difficult to reach – a view endorsed, among others, by Spanish educator Jose Luis Garcia and education technology researcher Sugata Mitra. Mitra's Granny Cloud concept relies heavily on communication tools such as Skype to connect schoolchildren in remote regions with retired people, who can encourage, nurture and guide them from a distance.[3]

I posted a Twitter question to my PLN of educators asking for people's views on the future of teaching. From those who responded there was a unanimous view that there will be a sea change in the way teachers conduct themselves in education, and that teachers will drive these changes.

Heidi Siwak, a Grade 6 teacher in Canada, predicted: 'I'll spend very little time designing lessons and more time assisting students in meeting their own learning goals.' These sentiments are echoed by several others. Martin Homola in Slovakia said teachers will pay 'more attention to specific needs and interests of pupils. Less authority, more friendly older sibling approach. More discussion.' Jack Beaman from the UK wanted to see small groups and a scenario where top experts would 'use technology to reach the masses,

---

3   Sugata Mitra, *The Granny Cloud*. Available online at: http://grannycloud. wordpress.com/about/.

allowing people to dictate their own learning.' He envisaged an education provision that would be 'less top-down and more social'.

Another UK teacher, Sonia Cooper, believes there will be a more dialogic kind of pedagogy, with teachers 'hopefully talking less to the class, not imparting knowledge but guiding learners by asking the right questions'. She is clearly advocating a discursive, participative approach to education. She sees teacher tasks such as assessment (marking) being 'very different, with verbal feedback recorded and recognised as vital'. She also believes that feedback to students will be given using other digital tools.

One head teacher in the UK, Andy Hampton, believes that teachers will begin to teach and promote 'Junior PLNs' (professional learning networks) as university-style teaching filters down to schools. Ben Jones, another educator, sees the vital importance of learners taking centre stage, but warns that we should not confuse personalised learning with individualised learning. Personalised learning is where the learner takes control of their own learning, whereas individualised learning does not necessarily connote ownership.

From these views it would appear that future changes in education will come from teachers adopting new practices, where social learning comes to the fore, and where there is more negotiation of meaning through dialogue with learners. Linda Barron, a teacher in Australia, even goes as far as to suggest that collaboration should be so entrenched in future learning that it will be difficult to tell the teachers apart from the learners. Such changes will need to come through flexibility and personalisation of learning, which will also bring new technologies into play. Changes are coming. It will be best for all if the future of education is shaped by teachers and learners in partnership, rather than by our politicians.

A final word ...

For myself and for many others with one eye on the future of education, learning continues to evolve in directions that are both richly social and intensely personal. This may sound paradoxical, but essentially, with all the digital tools we now have at our disposal, we have unprecedented opportunities to connect and create with our own powerful social networks and personal webs. Alongside the new and emerging theories of pedagogy, educators have a powerful set of tools and ideas at their disposal.

In schools of the future, I believe that children will use personal technologies in a similar way to the way they now use pens and pencils. We will not be seeing ICT suites or computer labs in the future any more than we see pencil suites now. Education needs a seamless provision that blurs the boundaries between what children use to learn when they are inside school and when they are outside the school gates. Teachers need to engineer a culture where the excitement of informal learning and the powerful richness of social media, personal gaming and instant messaging can be just as successfully employed inside the formal learning space.

Educators also have the opportunity to take these tools and use them to create their own individual learning pathways, select their own personal preferences, and devise their own unique collections of resources for professional development. New theories can be applied to illuminate new learning, and help us all to discover some of the best ways we can harness the power of new technologies for education. What's more, we should be using the small device that fits in the palm of our hand to open up amazing new vistas of learning for ourselves, and for our students.

In other words, the future of learning – for a while at least – is going to be smart mobile. So the next time you go to text a friend or post a picture to Snapchat, remember …

You literally hold your future in your hands.

Bibliography

Agar, J. *Constant touch: A Global History of the Mobile Phone* (Cambridge: Icon Books, 2013).

Alexander, C., Ishikawa, S. and Silverstein, M. *A Pattern Language: Towns, Buildings, Construction* (Oxford: Oxford University Press, 1977).

Anderson, L. and Krathwohl, D. R. (eds.), *A Taxonomy for Learning, Teaching and Assessing: A Revision of Bloom's Taxonomy of Educational Objectives* (London: Longman, 2001).

Applebee, A. N. *Curriculum as Conversation: Transforming Traditions of Teaching and Learning* (Chicago: University of Chicago Press, 1996).

Arkell, H. 'Coroner Warns of Dangers of Facebook', Mail Online. Available online at: http://www.dailymail.co.uk/news/article-2513782/Facebook-bullies-led-suicide-student-19-hanged-himself.html.

Bandura, A. 'Social Learning' in Antony S. R. Manstead and Miles Hewstone (eds.) *The Blackwell Encyclopedia of Social Psychology* (Blackwell Publishing, 1999): 576–581.

Baudelaire, C. *The Painter of Modern Life and Other Essays* (New York: Da Capo Press, 1964).

Beishuizen, J. 'Does a Community of Learners Foster Self-Regulated Learning?' *Technology, Pedagogy and Education* 17,3 (2008); 183–193.

Bennett, S., Maton, K. and Kervin, L. 'The 'Digital Natives' Debate: A Critical Review of the Evidence', *British Journal of Educational Technology*, 39, 5 (2008): 775–786.

Bergmann, J. and Sams, A. 'Flipping the Classroom', *Tech & Learning* 32.10 (2012): 42–43.

Bleakley, A. 'Curriculum as Conversation', *Advances in Health Sciences Education* 14.3 (2009): 297–301.

Bloom, B. S. and Krathwohl, D. R. *Taxonomy of Educational Objectives: The Classification of Educational Goals, Handbook I: Cognitive Domain* (New York: Longmans, 1956).

Bloom, B. S., Krathwohl, D. R. and Masia, B. B. *Taxonomy of Educational Objectives: The Classification of Educational Goals, Handbook II: Affective Domain* (New York: David McKay Company, 1964).

Boud, D., Keogh, R. and Walker, D. *Reflection: Turning Experience into Learning* (Abingdon: Routledge, 1985): 52–68.

Brabazon, T. *Digital Hemlock* (Sydney: University of New South Wales Press, 2002).

Brabazon, T. *The University of Google: Education in the (Post) Information Age* (Aldershot: Ashgate Publishing Ltd, 2012).

Braverman, H. *Labor and Monopoly Capital* (New York: Monthly Review Press, 1974).

Bruner, J. S. *Actual Minds, Possible Worlds* (Cambridge MA: Harvard University Press, 2009).

Burvall, A. YouTube History Teachers Channel, 2013. Available online at: https://www.youtube.com/user/historyteachers.

Carr, N. *The Shallows: What the Internet is Doing to Our Brains* (New York: W. W. Norton & Company, 2011).

Carr, W. and Kemmis, S. *Becoming Critical: Education, Knowledge and Action Research* (London: Routledge, 2003).

Clark, A. *Natural Born Cyborgs: Minds, Technologies and the Future of Human Intelligence* (Oxford: Oxford University Press, 2003).

Cooley, C. *Human Nature and the Social Order* (New York: Scribner, 1902).

Cormier, D. 'Rhizomatic Education: Community as Curriculum' (2008). Available online at: http://davecormier.com/edblog/2008/06/03/rhizomatic-education-community-as-curriculum/.

Corneli, J. 'Paragogical Praxis', *e-Learning and Digital Media* 9.3 (2012): 267–272.

Corneli, J. and Danoff, C. J. 'Paragogy', OKCon (2011).

Crook, C. and Harrison, C. *Web 2.0 Technologies for Learning at Key Stages 3 and 4* (Coventry: Becta Publications, 2008).

Cross, J. *Informal Learning* (Hoboken NJ: John Wiley & Sons, 2006).

Crystal, D. *Txtng: The Gr8 Db8* (Oxford: Oxford University Press, 2008).

Csíkszentmihályi, Mihályi *Flow: The Psychology of Optimal Experience* (New York: Harper & Row, 1990).

Cuban, L. *Oversold and Underused: Computers in the Classroom* (Cambridge MA: Harvard University Press, 2009).

Curtis, M. *Distraction: Being Human in the Digital Age* (London: Futuretext, 2004).

Curtis, S. 'Digital Learning: How Technology is Reshaping Teaching'. *The Telegraph*, 23 August 2014. Available online at: http://www.telegraph.co.uk/technology/news/11051228/Digital-learning-how-technology-is-reshaping-teaching.html.

Davidson, C. N. *Now You See It: How Technology and Brain Science Will Transform Schools and Business for the 21st Century* (New York: Viking, 2011).

Deleuze, G. and Guattari, F. *A Thousand Plateaus: Capitalism and Schizophrenia* (London: Bloomsbury Publishing, 1988).

Delfino, M., Dettori G. and Persico, D. 'Self-Regulated Learning in Virtual Communities', *Technology, Pedagogy and Education* 17.3 (2008): 195–205.

Demos, *About Learning. Report of the Learning Working Group* (London: Demos, 2004).

Department for Education, *The National Strategies. National Archives.* Available online at: http://webarchive.nationalarchives.gov.uk/20131216163513/https://www.education.gov.uk/schools/toolsandinitiatives/nationalstrategies.

Dewey, J. *How We Think* (Boston: Heath, 1933).

Engeström, Y. 'Activity Theory and Individual and Social Transformation', *Perspectives on Activity Theory* (1999): 19–38.

Federman, M. 'Organization Effectiveness and Leadership Development: What is the (Next) Message' (2010). Available online at: http://whatisthemessage.blogspot.co.uk/2010_08_01_archive.html.

Festinger, L. 'A Theory of Social Comparison Processes', *Human Relations* 7.2 (1954): 117–140.

Fiore, Q. and McLuhan, M. *The Medium is the Massage* (New York: Random House, 1967).

Freire, P. *Pedagogy of the Oppressed* (London: Bloomsbury Publishing, 2000).

Garcia, J. L. *Didactics: Higher Education and Teacher Training* [blog]. Available online at: http://nnttunican.blogspot.com/.

Gee, J. P. *What Video Games Have to Teach Us About Learning and Literacy* (New York: Palgrave Macmillan, 2003).

Gerver, R. *Creating Tomorrow's Schools Today* (London: Continuum Press, 2011).

Goffman, E. 'Role-distance', in Brisset, D. and Edgley, C. (eds.) *Life as Theater: A Dramaturgical Sourcebook,* (Chicago: Aldine Publishing Company, 1961): 123–132.

Goldsworthy, S., Lawrence, N. and Goodman, W. 'The Use of Personal Digital Assistants at the Point of Care in an Undergraduate Nursing Program', *Computers Informatics Nursing* 24.3 (2006): 138–143.

Goodfellow, R. 'Scholarly, Digital, Open: an Impossible Triangle?' *Research in Learning Technology* 21 (2014). Available online at: http://dx.doi.org/10.3402/rlt. v21.21366.

Greenfield, S. *The Quest For Identity In The 21st Century* (London: Sceptre, 2009).

Hase, S. and Kenyon, C. 'Heutagogy: A Child of Complexity Theory', *Complicity: An International Journal of Complexity and Education* 4.1 (2007).

Heick, T. '12 Principles of Mobile Learning', TeachThought Blog (2012). Available online at: http://www.teachthought.com/ technology/12-principles-of-mobile-learning/.

Heppell, S. 'Good Tested Ideas to Transform Learning' (2014). Available online at: http://www.pinterest.com/stephenheppell/ good-tested-ideas-to-transform-learning/.

Hillman, D., Willis, D. and Gunawardena, C. 'Learner Interface Interaction in Distance Education', *The American Journal of Distance Education* 8.2 (1994).

Honey, P. and Mumford, A. *Using Your Learning Styles* (Maidenhead: Peter Honey, 1986).

Huggett, S. 'Learning to Rewrite History', *SQ Magazine*, 9 September, 2011. Available online at: http://sqmagazine.co.uk/2011/09/ feature-learning-to-rewrite-history/.

Illich, I. *Deschooling Society* (London: Penguin, 1971).

Illich, I. *Tools for Conviviality* (New York: Harper and Row, 1973).

Jeffs, M. and Smith, T. *Learning from Experience* (1999). Available online at: http:// www.infed.org/foundations/f-explrn.htm.

John, P. and Wheeler, S. *The Digital Classroom* (London: Routledge, 2008).

Jonassen, D. H. *Computers in the Classroom: Mindtools for Critical Thinking* (Englewood Cliffs NJ: Prentice-Hall, 1996).

Jonassen, D. H., Peck, K. and Wilson, B. *Learning with Technology: A Constructivist Perspective* (Under Saddle River: Merrill Prentice Hall, 1999).

Jones, C. and Healing, G. 'Net Generation Students: Agency and Choice and the New Technologies', *Journal of Computer Assisted Learning,* 26.3 (2010): 344–356.

Keen, A. *The Cult of the Amateur* (New York: Doubleday, 2007).

Kemp, C. 'What is School? Creating Change in Education.' Professional Reflection Blog (28 August 2014). Available online at: http://mrkempnz.com/2014/08/ what-is-school-creating-change-in-education.html.

Kennedy, G., Judd, T., Dalgarnot, B. and Waycott, J. 'Beyond Digital Natives and Immigrants: Exploring Types of Net Generation Students', *Journal of Computer Assisted Learning,* 26.5 (2010): 332–343.

Kolb, D. A. *Experiential Learning: Experience as the Source of Learning and Development* (Englewood Cliffs NJ: Prentice-Hall, 1984).

Kress, G. *Literacy in the New Media Age* (London: Routledge, 2009).

Krotoski, A. 'Storytelling: Digital Technology Allows us to Tell Tales in Innovative New Ways', *The Guardian*, 7 August, 2011. Available online at: http://www. theguardian.com/technology/2011/aug/07/digital-media-storytelling-internet.

Kurzweil, R. 'The Accelerating Power of Technology', TED Talks (2005). Available online at: https://www.ted.com/talks/ray_kurzweil_on_how_technology_will_transform_us.

Lankshear, C. and Knobel, M. *New Literacies: Everyday Practice and Classroom Learning* (New York: McGraw Hill, 2006).

Lima, M. 'Royal Society of Arts Animate: The Power of Networks' (2012). Available online at: https://www.youtube.com/watch?v=nJmGrNdJ5Gw.

Livingstone, S. *Children and the Internet* (Oxford: Polity Press, 2009).

Martin, F. G. 'Will Massive Open Online Courses Change How We Teach?' *Communications of the ACM* 55.8 (2012): 26–28.

Maslow, A. H. *Motivation and Personality* (New York: Harper, 1954).

Mayes, T. and de Freitas, S. 'Review of e-Learning Theories, Frameworks and Models', *JISC e-Learning Models Desk Study* 1 (2004).

McLuhan, M. *Understanding Media: The Extensions of Man* (Chicago: MIT Press, 1994).

Merrick, R. 'Choose Your Own Flight Path', Inspiration Engineering, 16 July, 2011. Available online at: http://inspirationengineering.com/2011/07/16/534/.

Mitra, S. *The Granny Cloud*. Available online at: http://grannycloud.wordpress.com/about/.

Moore, M. G. 'Editorial: Three types of interaction', *The American Journal of Distance Education*, 3, 2: (1989).

Moravec, J. W. (ed.), *Knowmad Society* (Minneapolis: Education Futures, 2013). Available online at: http://www.knowmadsociety.com/download/.

Nelson, T. and Narens, L. 'Metamemory: A Theoretical Framework and New Findings', in G. H. Bower (ed.), *The Psychology of Learning and Motivation* (New York: Academic Press, 1990): 125–141.

Oblinger, D. 'Boomers, Gen-xers, and Millennials: Understanding the New Students', *Educause Review*. 38.4 (2003).

Ormell, C. P. 'Bloom's Taxonomy and the Objectives of Education', *Educational Research* 17 (1974).

Overbaugh, R. C. and Schultz, L. 'Bloom's Taxonomy' (2005). Available online at: http://ww2.odu.edu/educ/roverbau/Bloom/blooms_taxonomy.htm.

Palfrey, J. and Gasser, U. *Born Digital: Understanding the First Generation of Digital Natives* (New York: Basic Books, 2008).

Papert, S. *Mindstorms: Children, Computers and Powerful Ideas* (Brighton: Harvester Press, 1980).

Paris, S. G., Byrnes, J. P. and Paris, A. H. 'Constructing Theories, Identities, and Actions of Self-Regulated Learners', *Self-Regulated Learning and Academic Achievement: Theoretical Perspectives* 2 (2001): 253–287.

Paton, G. 'Grand Theft Auto Used to Turn Children Against Crime', *The Telegraph*, 9 April, 2011.

Piaget, J. 'Piaget's Theory' in P. Mussen (ed.), *Carmichael's Manual of Child Psychology, Vol. 1* (Hoboken NJ: John Wiley & Sons, 1970): 703–732.

Pontefract, D. *Flat Army: Creating a Connected and Engaged Organization* (Hoboken NJ: Jossey-Bass, 2013).

Prensky, M. 'Digital Natives, Digital Immigrants', *On the Horizon* 9.5 (2001).

PRWeb UK, 'Children in Malawi Triple Maths Knowledge in Just Eight Weeks Using EuroTalk Apps' (December 2013). Available online at: http://uk.prweb.com/releases/EuroTalk/Malawi/prweb11433155.htm.

Quinlan, O. 'Bringing Theory and Practice to Teaching' (2012). Available online at: http://www.oliverquinlan.com/blog/2012/10/23/praxis-bringing-theory-and-practice-to-teaching/.

Rheingold, H. *Smart Mobs: The Next Social Revolution* (New York: Basic Books, 2007).

Robinson, K. 'How Schools Kill Creativity', TED Talks (2006). Available online at: http://www.ted.com/talks/ken_robinson_says_schools_kill_creativity.

Robinson, K. 'How to Escape Education's Death Valley', TED Talks (April 2013). Available online at: http://www.ted.com/talks/ken_robinson_how_to_escape_education_s_death_valley.

Rose, F. *The Art of Immersion: How the Digital Generation is Remaking Hollywood, Madison Avenue and the Way We Tell Stories* (New York: W. W. Norton & Company, 2010).

Rushkoff, D. *Playing the Future: What We Can Learn from Digital Kids* (London: HarperCollins, 1996).

Ryberg, T. and Christiansen, E. 'Community and Social Network Sites as Technology Enhanced Learning Environments', *Technology, Pedagogy and Education* 17 (3) (2008): 207–220.

Selwyn, N. 'The Digital Native: Myth and Reality', *Aslib Proceedings* 61.4 (2011): 364-379.

Shirky, C. *Cognitive Surplus: Creativity and Generosity in a Connected Age* (London: Penguin, 2010).

Shirky, C. *Here Comes Everybody: The Power of Organizing without Organizations* (London: Penguin, 2008).

Shortis, T. *The Language of ICT: Information and Communication Technology* (New York: Psychology Press, 2001).

Siemens, G. *Connectivism* (2002). Available online at: http://www.elearnspace.org/.

Smith, M. K. *David A. Kolb on Experiential Learning* (2001). Available online at: http://www.infed.org/biblio/b-explrn.htm.

Spencer, J. T. 'Bloom's Taxonomy: Criticisms. Teacher Commons' (2008). Available online at: http://teachercommons.blogspot.co.uk/2008/04/bloom-taxonomy-criticisms.html.

Steffens, K. 'Technology Enhanced Learning Environments for Self-Regulated Learning: A Framework for Research', *Technology, Pedagogy and Education* 17.3 (2008): 221–232.

Sugrue, B. 'Problems with Bloom's Taxonomy' (2002). Available online at: http://eppicinc.files.wordpress.com/2011/08/sugrue_bloom_critique_perfxprs.pdf.

Surowiecki, J. *The Wisdom of Crowds: Why the Many are Smarter than the Few and How Collective Wisdom Shapes Business, Economies, Societies and Nations* (New York: Abacus, 2010).

Tapscott, D. *Growing up Digital: The Rise of the Net Generation* (New York: McGraw Hill, 1998).

Thomas, D. and Seely Brown, J. *A New Culture of Learning: Cultivating the Imagination for a World of Constant Change* (CreateSpace, 2011).

Thomas, S., Joseph, C., Lacetti, J., Mason, B., Mills, B. S., Perril, S. and Pullinger, K. 'Transliteracy: Crossing Divides', *First Monday* 12 (2007): 3.

Toffler, A. *Future Shock* (New York: Random House, 1990).

Turkle, S. *Life on Screen: Identity in the Age of the Internet* (Simon & Schuster, 1995).

Vaidhyanathan, S. 'Generational Myth: Not all Young People are Tech-Savvy', *The Chronicle of Higher Education* 55(4) (2008).

Veen, W. and Vrakking, B. *Homo Zappiens: Growing up in a Digital Age* (London: Network Continuum Education, 2006).

Vygotsky, L. *Mind in Society: The Development of Higher Psychological Processes* (Cambride MA: Harvard University Press, 1980).

Wheeler, D. 'Digital Tribes, Virtual Clans', in S. Wheeler (ed.), *Connected Minds, Emerging Cultures* (Charlotte NC: Information Age, 2009): 65–76.

Wheeler, S. 'Teaching with Twitter', Learning with 'e's (2009). Available online at: http://steve-wheeler.blogspot.com/2009/01/teaching-with-twitter.html.

Wheeler, S. 'Two Fingered Salute', Learning with 'e's (2009). Available online at: http://steve-wheeler.blogspot.com/2009/08/two-fingered-salute.html.

Wheeler, S. 'Connected Educators', Learning with 'e's (2011). Available online at: http://steve-wheeler.blogspot.com/2011/11/connected-educators.html.

Wheeler, S. 'Using Wikis in Teacher Education' in M. Lee and C. McLoughlin (eds.) *Web 2.0-Based e-Learning: Applying Social Informatics for Tertiary Teaching* (Sydney: IGI Global, 2011): 180–191.

Wheeler, S. 'GRIN and Bear it: Our Transhumanist Futures', Learning with 'e's (2014). Available online at: http://steve-wheeler.blogspot.co.uk/2013/06/grin-and-bear-it.html.

Wheeler, S. 'A Day in the Life: The Quantified Self', Learning with 'e's (2014). Available online at: http://steve-wheeler.blogspot.co.uk/2014/02/a-day-in-life-quantified-self.html.

Wheeler, S. and Keegan, H. 'Imagined Worlds, Emerging Cultures', in S. Wheeler (ed.), *Connected Minds, Emerging Cultures* (Charlotte NC: Information Age, 2009): 261–276.

Wheeler, S. and Malik, M. 'Personal Learning Environments: A Bridge in the Cloud?' Paper presented at the 1st PLE Conference, Barcelona, 2011.

Wheeler, S., Yeomans, P. and Wheeler, D. 'The Good, the Bad and the Wiki: Evaluating student-generated content for collaborative learning', *British Journal of Educational Technology* 39.6 (2008): 987–995.

White, D. and Le Cornu, A. 'Visitors and Residents: A New Typology for Online Engagement', *First Monday* 16.9 (2011). Available online at: http://firstmonday.org/ojs/index.php/fm/article/view/3171.

Wikipedia, 'Criterion-Referenced Test'. Available online at: http://en.wikipedia.org/wiki/Criterion-referenced_assessment.

Wikipedia, 'Ipsative Assessment'. Available online at: http://en.wikipedia.org/wiki/Ipsative.

Woodruff, P. 'Socratic Education', *Philosophers on Education*, 1998: 14–31.

Wright, S. 'Flipping Bloom's Taxonomy' (2012). Available online at: http://plpnetwork.com/2012/05/15/flipping-blooms-taxonomy/.

Young, C. A. 'Conversation as Curriculum: Learning to Teach English in Rural America', *English Journal* (2004): 82–88.

Index

Y

Z